Frogs and snails
and
feminist tales

D0977707

Frogs and snails AND Feminist TALES

Preschool children and gender

BRONWYN DAVIES

Sydney
ALLEN & UNWIN
Wellington London Boston

First published in 1989
Allen & Unwin Australia Pty Ltd
An Unwin Hyman company
8 Napier Street, North Sydney NSW 2059 Australia

Allen & Unwin New Zealand Limited
75 Ghuznee Street, Wellington, New Zealand

Unwin Hyman Limited
15–17 Broadwick Street, London W1V 1FP, England

Unwin Hyman Inc.
8 Winchester Place, Winchester, Mass 01890 USA

National Library of Australia
Cataloguing-in-Publication entry: Davies, Bronwyn, 1945–
  Frogs and snails and feminist tales: preschool
  children and gender.

  Bibliography.
  Includes index.
  ISBN 0 04 520007 6.

  1. Sex differences (Psychology) in children. 2. Sex
  role in children. 3. Child rearing. I. Title.

155.4'23

Library of Congress Catalog Card Number: 89–83596
Set in 10/11pt Times by Setrite Typesetters, Hong Kong
Printed in Hong Kong by Dah Hua Printing Co Ltd.

Contents

Acknowledgements

I would like to thank the following friends and colleagues for their comments on various drafts of this book: Caroline Baker, Kerry Dunne, Rom Harré, Frigga Haug, Margo Huxley, Lesley Rogers, Margaret Somerville and Valerie Walkerdine. I would also like to thank Nancy Holden for the video-camera work, Sushma Dua and Mary Henry for their work in transcribing the audio-tapes, and my son Paul who did all the cooking and housekeeping while I was writing this book. Special thanks, of course, must go to the children who took part in the study.

Permissions

The author acknowledges with thanks permission to reproduce material as follows: sections of the text of *The Paper Bag Princess*, the publishers Annick Press Ltd, Canada, and the author, Robert N. Munsch; the illustration on the front cover and p. 65, the publishers Annick Press Ltd, Canada, and the illustrator, Michael Martchenko. *The Paper Bag Princess*, © 1980 was published by Annick Press Ltd in Canada and is distributed by Firefly Books Ltd in the US, Hippo Books in the UK and Ashton Scholastic in Australia.

Introduction

Two events inspired this book. The first was associated with the story *The Paper Bag Princess*. This is an amusing story about a princess called Elizabeth who goes to incredible lengths to save her prince from a fierce dragon. At the beginning of the story, Princess Elizabeth and Prince Ronald are planning to get married, but then the dragon comes along, burns Elizabeth's castle and clothes and flies off into the distance carrying Prince Ronald by the seat of his pants. Elizabeth is very angry. She finds a paper bag to wear and follows the dragon. She tricks him into displaying all of his magic powers until he falls asleep from exhaustion. She rushes into the dragon's cave to save Ronald only to find that he does not want to be saved by a princess who is covered in soot and only has an old paper bag to wear. Elizabeth is quite taken aback by this turn of events, and she says: 'Ronald, your clothes are really pretty and your hair is very neat. You look like a real prince, but you are a bum.' The last page shows her skipping off into the sunset alone and the story ends with the words: 'They didn't get married after all.'

When I first encountered this story in the home of a friend, I read it to her five-year-old daughter whenever I had the opportunity. But I noticed that she did not appreciate it in the same way that I did, and I began to notice that she looked at me as if I were odd when I suggested we read it. I then began to talk to her about the story, and discovered that the meanings which seemed to me to be readily available to any listener were not necessarily available to her, that the story she was hearing was different from the one that I was hearing (see Adams, 1986).

The second event also involved the same five-year-old. The scene was a gathering of friends and their children on a picnic in a nearby forest. There was a child there whom neither she nor I had met before. The straw-like unkempt hair, old jeans and checked shirt, the rough way of talking and eating, left us in no doubt that this was a boy. When someone who knew her called her Penny, I was startled, but my five-year-old friend was shocked and outraged. She asked her mother to take her to the toilet, and when they were out of earshot she asked her, with tears in her eyes, 'Mummy why are they calling that boy Penny!' The disturbance that she felt seemed to be related not so much to the failure on her part to read Penny 'correctly', that is, as a girl (since she still presumed that Penny was a boy), but to the fact that others could give a boy a girl's name. Such an action appeared to generate in her a deep sense of moral outrage.

What is so important, I wondered, about getting one's own and other people's gender right? Why does it matter so much? Why was it that Penny, far from being a source of sheer delight to those who encountered her, impressed with her ability to cast off feminine stereotypes, was regarded as a problem? Why did the ways of being that she adopted have to be negotiated and struggled over? Why did she have to exaggerate her 'maleness' to the extent that she had? Why were other parents critical of the fact that she was dressed the way she was, and that her hair looked like straw, when they probably would not even have noticed the condition of her hair and her clothes if she had been a boy? And on the other side, why was it that parents and preschool teachers who were interested in raising and teaching children in a non-sexist way were forever commenting that, despite their best efforts, girls seemed to be very much into being little girls and boys into being boys?

I decided to find more feminist stories, and to begin a systematic exploration of young children's understanding of them. In the first stage of the study I chose eight children from varied backgrounds, and spent hundreds of hours reading the stories to them individually. Each reading was recorded and transcribed, and the children's comments studied in detail in order to discover the way in which they were making sense of what they heard. I then decided to spend some time in preschools observing children playing as well as reading them stories so that I could fit children's understanding of the stories to their actions in the everyday world. In this second stage I recorded readings of stories with more than 40 children.

After two years of collecting such data in Armidale, Sydney and Melbourne, and with the aid of poststructuralist theory to make sense of my data, I began to feel that I could grasp what was going on in those early incidents which sparked off the study. The taking on of traditional forms of femininity or masculinity was no mere individual whim on the part of each child, nor was it that parents were pressing their children into particular ways of being male and female. It was the incorrigibility of the male−female dualism and its construction as a central element of human identity that was the problem.

Adults interested in liberating children from oppressive sex roles are generally not questioning maleness and femaleness as such.

They are simply rejecting the negative side of femininity for girls (fragility, timidity, obsession with appearance and with domesticity), and the negative side of masculinity for boys (aggression, insensitivity, rudeness and a refusal to be helpful). What we have failed to realise in wondering why it is that children so enthusiastically take up these ways of being so is that these qualities themselves are key signifiers of dualistic maleness and femaleness. Children cannot both be required to position themselves as identifiably male or female and at the same time be deprived of the means of signifying maleness and femaleness, Yet this is what the vast majority of non-sexist programs have expected them to do.

The incorrigibility of the male—female dualism

Part of being a competent member of society as it is currently organised derives from our capacity to attribute to others, and to aid others in attributing to us, the 'correct' gender. Everyone 'knows' that the world is divided into males and females. The idea that there are two sexes, and only two, and that they are antithetical, bipolar opposites, is an incorrigible proposition within Western thought (Mehan and Wood, 1975). Kessler and McKenna point out that:

> As we go about our daily lives, we assume that every human being is either a male or a female. We make this assumption for everyone who ever lived and for every future human being ... It is [taken to be] a fact that someone is a man or a woman, just as it is a fact that the result of a coin toss is either heads or tails, and we can easily decide the case by looking. (Kessler and McKenna, 1978: 1)

But this assumption, I will argue, is a byproduct, as well as an underlying assumption, of the social and linguistic structures through which individuals constitute themselves as persons. The meaning that we give to being male or female in the everyday world rests on the assumption of bipolarity of physiological difference which serves as the ground on which bipolar social selves are constituted. This construction has been aided by a great deal of faulty 'science' which has *assumed* bipolar physiological difference and set out to 'prove' that the bipolarity of gendered selves stems from that physiological bipolarity (Connell, 1987; Rogers, 1975, 1981, 1988).

The position I will put forward in this book is that children learn to take up their maleness or femaleness as if it were an incorrigible element of their personal and social selves, and that they do so through learning the discursive practices in which all people are positioned as either male or female. By basing our interactions with children on the presumption that they are in some unitary and bipolar sense male or female, we teach them the discursive practices through which they can constitute themselves in that way.

In what follows I have set out to analyse the way in which the dualistic gender order is experienced by preschool children. To the extent that I have successfully mapped out what is going on in the processes whereby children are constituted as male or female, then I have opened up the possibility for programes of change that may genuinely work.

A brief note on poststructuralist theory

Poststructuralist theory, with its roots in Freud, Marx and Foucault, provides a radical framework for understanding the relation between persons and their social world and for conceptualising social change. The structures and processes of the social world are recognised as having a material force, a capacity to constrain, to shape, to coerce, as well as to potentiate individual action. The processes whereby individuals take themselves up as persons are understood as ongoing processes. The individual is not so much a social construction which results in some relatively fixed end product, but one who is constituted and reconstituted through a variety of discursive practices. It is the recognition of the ongoing nature of the constitution of self and the recognition of the nonunitary nature of self that makes poststructuralist theory different from social construction theory.

Individuals, through learning the discursive practices of a society, are able to position themselves within those practices in multiple ways, and to develop subjectivities both in concert with and in opposition to the ways in which others choose to position them. By focusing on the multiple subject positions that a person takes up and the often contradictory nature of those positionings, and by focusing on the fact that the social world is constantly being constituted through the discursive practices in which individuals engage, we are able to see individuals not as the unitary beings that humanist theory would have them be, but as the complex, changing, contradictory creatures that we each experience ourselves to be, despite our best efforts at producing a unified, coherent and relatively static self.

If we see society as being constantly created through discursive practices then it is possible to see the power of those practices, not only to create and sustain the social world but also to see how we can change that world through a refusal of certain discourses and the generation of new ones.

Poststructuralist theory is itself a discourse that we can take up. I choose to take it up here because it provides me with the conceptual tools to make sense of my data and allows me to formulate answers to the questions that I set out with. It is a radical discourse because it allows us to think beyond the male−female dualism as inevitable, to the constitutive processes through which we position ourselves as male or female and which we can change if we so choose.

Becoming male or female

In order to become recognisable and acceptable members of the society they are born into, children must learn to think with and act in terms of the accepted, known linguistic forms. This is not just a skill they must acquire in order to communicate, but an acquisition of the means by which they constitute themselves as persons in relation to others in the social world. In learning the language they learn to constitute themselves and others as unitary beings, as capable of coherent thought, as gendered, and as one who is in particular kinds of relation to others. Language is both a resource and a constraint. It makes social and personal being possible but it also limits the available forms of being to those which make sense within the terms provided by the language. In the words of Black and Coward (1981) '. . . language has a material existence. It defines our possibilities and limitations, it constitutes our subjectivities' (cited in Lees, 1986b; 159; see also Threadgold, 1988).

Usually we think of the passing on of linguistic skills to children as unproblematic except where there is some kind of failure to pass them on. Language is a necessary tool for survival in the social world. But language also provides the tools and the materials with which the social structure is created and maintained. In passing language on to children we also pass on a relative entrapment in the social order, including those elements of the social order we might well want to move beyond.

Adults require children to adopt their linguistic practices, not just for the child's own benefit but as a way of confirming the rightness of the world as they understand it. Until children have accepted the terms of reference embedded in the language, they are potentially a disruptive force, undermining 'what adults claim is "obvious" and "known" to "everybody"' (Waksler, 1986: 74).

Part of what is 'obvious and known to everybody' is that people

1

are either male or female. In learning the discursive practices of their society children learn that they must be socially identifiable as one or the other, even though there is very little if any observable physical difference in most social situations. Dress, hairstyle, speech patterns and content, choice of activity—all become key signifiers that can be used in successfully positioning oneself as a girl or a boy.

Correct positioning is facilitated by the interactive others each child encounters and by the discursive practices they learn in which bipolar maleness and femaleness are embedded. I once gave a toy car to a three-year-old girl as a symbolic refusal of the gender order. She unwrapped the present, looked at me quizzically and said, 'It's really a boy's toy, but don't worry, I can handle it', at one and the same time reconstituting the gender order that I was attempting to break down, and taking care, as girls should, not to hurt my feelings too much at having my error pointed out to me. A similar gesture with a three-year-old boy, when I gave him a music box, simply resulted in a sulky refusal to interact with me or the music box— how can one, he may well have asked, interact with adults who refuse to cooperate with the establishment of one's correct gendered positioning?

Of course taking oneself up as a boy or a girl is not a unitary process. How one 'does' masculinity or femininity with one's parents, say, may differ profoundly from how one 'does' masculinity with one's friends, or from one friend to another. A fascinating episode that I became involved in quite by chance during the period that I was undertaking this study illustrates the coercive nature of adult discourse in relation to children. It also shows how children learn both to position themselves to advantage within that discourse and to develop quite a different discourse for use with each other in the absence of adults.

The episode took place when I accepted a lift in the car of an acquaintance who was on her way to pick her children up from an elite private boy's school. The boys, two brothers aged five and seven, and a friend aged seven, were waiting quietly with their peers and their teachers in a rain shelter at the front of the school as the mothers drove up in their Porsches and Mercedes. The scene was very orderly with each boy neatly attired in a yellow raincoat and rain hat. As each mother drove up, the required routine was that each child say 'good afternoon' to his teacher, or shake her hand, and then climb without haste into his mother's car. The boys jumped into the back seat (I was in the front) and the five-year-old announced that he hadn't said good afternoon to his teacher. His mother observed that he would be in trouble tomorrow. The children were each introduced to me. They greeted me very politely, seat belts were fastened and we drove off. The mother asked them about what had happened at school that day and managed to elicit almost no information other than whether they had played inside or outside at lunchtime. The children were nevertheless very 'well spoken' and polite. There was some friction between the parent and the youngest child when he took off his seat belt in order to remove his raincoat. She pointed out that she would, as she had on previous occasions, stop the car, even though we were on a freeway, if he did not immediately fasten his seat belt. She pointed out that this would be to the great irritation of the other drivers. He fastened his seat belt.

The day was overcast and hot, and the heater in the car was full on. The conversation turned to which games they would play when they got home and what they would have to eat. A potential conflict between whether they would play table tennis or model trains ensued. The mother announced that the youngest child, who asked for table tennis, had first choice as he had asked first. The other two quietly discussed how he was going to be able to play table tennis if they would not play with him, and the mother counteracted this by saying that she would play with him. They decided to play table tennis today and trains tomorrow. It was a long, hot drive and I was amazed at how quiet and polite the children were, especially given the discomfort they must have felt in their sweaty raincoats. I began to wonder whether these boys were in fact different from any of the other boys I had worked with, and whether this had something to do with their class membership. Eventually we stopped and the mother got out to go to the bank, leaving me and the boys in the car. They immediately adopted a totally different way of behaving, and I, as stranger, was totally ignored. They pressed all the buttons in the car, they romped, they threw their raincoats off, and then they started a wild game which involved grabbing each other's genitals. There was a noisy mixture of pleasurable squeals of laughter and screams of pain. They jockeyed for power, for control, for an ally, not to be one against two and not to be hurt too much. It was wild and exciting and painful. After ten minutes or so of this riotous and noisy behaviour I spotted the mother coming back and told them so. They settled down rapidly. When she got into the car she asked me had they been behaving themselves. There was a tense pause and then I said, 'They were delightful'. One of the boys said 'thankyou' with obvious relief in his voice, charming and polite, entirely relocated as child in the particular form of adult−child discourse that he clearly knew well.

There was a little bit of wriggling in the back as we took off, and the youngest child whinged in a pathetic voice to his mother that one of the others was pushing him. Power now resided not in who was smartest at grabbing whose genitals and in protecting his own, but on who could get his mother on side, and off side with the other two. The transformation was profound and dramatic and the boys were completely in command of it, producing the small, sweet, powerless child required by their mother. Although the switch was almost automatic, it felt to me like an uncomfortable, somehow 'unreal' switch, not because of some lingering humanist presumptions about the unitary nature of the person, but because the extent to which they were so visibly 'under control', 'behaving themselves' seemed to rob them in some sense of their personhood. My sympathy with their 'wild' state, despite the fact that it had been excruciatingly noisy, probably had a lot to do with the similarities between adult—child and male—female relations. Children are defined as *other* to adults in much the same way that women are other to men. Children have to learn to be both outside adult discourse and to participate with adults both in terms of adult's concepts of children and of adult—child relations (Davies, 1982).

Much of the adult world is not consciously taught to children, is not contained in the *content* of their talk, but is embedded in the language, in the discursive practices and the social and narrative structures through which the child is constituted as a person, as a child and as male or female. Poststructuralist theory allows us to recognise that what children learn through the process of interacting in the everyday world is not a unitary, non-contradictory language and practice—and it is not a unitary identity that is created through those practices, as the example of the boys in the yellow raincoats makes clear. Rather, children learn to see and understand in terms of the multiple positionings and forms of discourse that are available to them. More, they learn the forms of desire and of power and powerlessness that are embedded in and made possible by the various discursive practices through which they position themselves and the positioned.

Children (like adults) may be positioned in many ways during any one day, sometimes powerful and sometimes powerless. At the same time, and contrary to much of our experience, a consistent thread running through our discursive practices is the idea of each person as unitary, coherent, non-contradictory and as fixed in certain ways (cf. Harré, 1985). One of these assumed points of fixity is sex/gender.

Sex-role socialisation theory

Being male or female sometimes seems to be taken on more enthusiastically by children than adults expect—one quite often hears parents saying with some regret or puzzlement that their daughter is a real little girl and insists on wearing pretty dresses, or that their son just *is* heavily masculine and aggressive, and was so right from the beginning, despite their discouragement. They claim that they have tried to teach their boys to be gentle and their girls to be assertive, and yet they have turned out like any other boy or girl.

Perhaps it is genetic, after all, they say. How else to explain how the supposedly all-powerful parent has had so little influence?

This puzzlement derives to a large extent from the commonsense but inaccurate theories most of us have about the relationship between the individual and the social structure. The commonly used terms 'socialisation' and 'sex-roles' are part of the linguistic paraphernalia that misleads us. As well, the conceptual division of the person into the biological self (sex) and the social self (gender), although generated through feminist discourse and serving a useful function at the time that it was generated, aids in the confusion that is involved here.

In sex-role socialisation theory the biological basis of sexual difference is assumed, and the 'roles' that children are taught by adults are a superficial social dressing laid over the 'real' biological difference. There is, in these two beliefs, a profound confusion about what a person really is, and about how she/he becomes so.

Within the sex-role socialisation model of the world the child is taught her or his sex-role by, usually, one central adult, but is also 'pressed' into maintenance of that role by a multitude of others (peers, media, etc.). There is no room in this model for the child as active agent, the child as theorist, recognising for him or herself the way the social world is organised. Nor is there acknowledgement of the child as implicated in the construction and maintenance of the social world through the very act of recognising it and through learning its discursive practices. The problems with socialisation theory and with the adherence to any theory which relies on the concept of role has been thoroughly analysed by Connell (1987); Davies (1982, 1988a); Baker and Davies (1989); Edwards (1983); Henriques at al (1984); Jackson (1982); Sepeier (1976); Stanley and Wise (1983); Waksler (1986); Walkerdine (1981), and Wyn (1986). What I will do here is reiterate some of those arguments which deconstruct sex-role socialisation theory, and at the same time provide a workable alternative so that we do not keep slipping back into an explanatory frame work that has itself become an essential part of the discourse through which sex differences are maintained.

Walkerdine's work constitutes a significant contribution to the development of the alternative model that I am seeking to elaborate in this book. She has pioneered the application of poststructuralist theory to the production of gender in educational and domestic settings. She argues that we need to shift the focus away from individual identity to relations of power and to the multiple subjectivities that are available to any one person within the discursive practices of our society:

> certain feminist accounts have used the psychological concepts of 'role' and 'stereotype' to understand women and girls as unitary subjects whose

5

economic dependence, powerlessness and physical weakness is reflected in their production as 'passive', 'weak', and 'dependent' individuals. While such accounts have been extremely important in helping to develop ... feminist practices, ... such analyses might not be as helpful as we had previously supposed ... [F]emale teachers and small girls ... are not unitary subjects uniquely positioned, but produced as a nexus of subjectivities, in relations of power which are constantly shifting, rendering them at one moment powerful and at another powerless. (Walkerdine, 1981: 14)

Within socialisation theory, in contrast, the person doing the socialising is understood as the active agent and the person being socialised is a passive recipient, the 'object' or the 'raw material of socialisation' who is pressed into a relatively fixed form (Davies, 1982; Waksler, 1986: 74). This is highly problematic as any adult who has attempted to 'socialise' a child knows. Children do not accept what adults tell them as having application to every aspect of their lives, nor that the way they do things is necessarily appropriate for them as children (see Bussey, 1986; Davies, 1982). It is not possible for children simply and straightforwardly to accept the world as it is told to them, not least because the difference between the 'real' and the 'ideal' world is often quite marked in adult–child discourse. 'Don't do as I do, do as I say' was one of my father's favourite sayings.

The appeal of socialisation theory stems in large part from its relation to the individualistic humanist theories of the person that are so much part of the modern social world. These theories of the person obscure our recognition of the complex and contradictory ways in which we are continually constituting and reconstituting ourselves and the social world through the various discourses in which we participate. According to Weedon:

> Humanist discourses presuppose an essence at the heart of the individual which is unique, fixed and coherent and which makes her what she *is*. The nature of this essence varies between different forms of humanist discourse. It may be the unified rational consciousness of liberal political philosophy, the essence of womanhood at the heart of much radical-feminist discourse or the true human nature, alienated by capitalism, which is the focus of humanist Marxism. Against this irreducible humanist essence of subjectivity, poststructuralism proposes a subjectivity which is precarious, contradictory and in process, constantly being reconstituted in discourse each time we speak. (Weedon, 1987:33)

As well, socialisation theory rests on popular notions of the child and of adult–child relations. A further attraction comes from the preference for cause-and-effect explanations in Western thought. If there are describable links between the way children are treated and the way they behave, then the treatment is perceived as having

6

caused their behaviour. Wex (1979), for example, cites the finding of Brunet and Lezine that mothers spend much less time feeding female babies (an average of 25 minutes) than they do feeding male babies (an average of 45 minutes) This is said to be as part of the process whereby boys are 'taught' to recognise their own needs and to expect that these will be met, and girls are 'taught' to fit in with others' agendas, recognising that that is the only way that their needs will be attended to. Women are thus, according to Wex: 'prepared in an "ideal" manner for our later role as girl-"friend", wife, child-bearer, mother and to be other helping hands of the patriarchy ... And this is possible only because we have been so well trained to ignore our self-perception and the perception of our own interests' (Wex, 1979: 321).

The use of the word 'train' is problematic here, since it implies the intentional passing on of forms of action from one to another, and I don't think it is reasonable to assume that mothers deliberately cut their daughters' feeding time short in order to teach them to be girls (though one of my friends *was* told by a hospital nurse not to attend to her crying baby because she was a girl and would therefore have to 'learn to wait'). Wex's posited connection is nevertheless a powerful one and may help us to articulate a significant element of each of our biographies, that is, we can use it to help 'make sense' of the ways in which boys come to experience themselves as agents and in which girls learn not to focus on their own self-interest. But the time spent feeding each child cannot itself be a cause. Feeding female babies for 25 minutes would mean something quite different if male babies were also fed for 25 minutes, and different again if male babies were fed for fifteen minutes. What probably *is* happening, though, is that male babies are gaining practice at positioning themselves as one who makes demands and can reasonably expect that they will be met, while female babies are gaining practice at positioning themselves as one who is vulnerable to the needs of the other.

Researchers working within the socialisation model are at risk of getting caught up in doing simplistic research to show the ways in which adults are at fault in *causing* narrow stereotypical behaviours in children (see, for example, Walum, 1977; Weitzman, 1979; Maccoby and Jacklin, 1974; Safilios-Rothschild, 1979). Others simply tack it on to descriptions of adult—child relations in the belief that they need some kind of theory to 'explain' their data (see, for example, The Anti-sexist Working Party, 1985, and Goldman and Goldman, 1982). Because the assumptions underlying the theory remain unexamined, researchers working in this paradigm rarely feel the need to do more than assert a causal link between observed adult and observed child behaviours or attributes (see. Kenway and Willis, 1986). But a straightforward causal link is impossible to demonstrate, given the complexity of the social world, the multiple and contradictory nature of social reality, and the fact of simultaneous accommodations and resistances.

When this direct causal link cannot be demonstrated the second string of socialisation theory is called on. Using the conceptual division between sex and gender, we appeal to the biological as the 'real' cause of the child's behaviour and thus fall into a form of biological determinism. But the old assumptions we used to make about physiology are being seriously undermined by current biological research.

The place of biology in the creation of males and females

Although biologists have now found that genetic, hormonal and genital sex are not necessarily linked, there is still a lot of popular science around that not only links them together, but further links brain structure and behaviour in the everyday world. One reason it has been easy for scientists to make such linkages is that our linguistic structure encourages it. We only have bipolar words, such as 'boy' and 'girl', 'male' and 'female', 'man', and 'woman', to encompass genetic, hormonal, genital and social difference. The language suggests that they belong together in a unitary bipolar package—that if one has female genitals one will also have female genetic structure and a predominance of female hormones; and that if one has male genitals one will have male genetic structure and a predominance of male hormones. It is easy then to presume a mapping of behaviour onto physiological structure. It is not until recently that biologists have discovered that these different elements of maleness and femaleness don't necessarily belong together in a bipolar arrangement.

Kessler and McKenna (1978) point out that every characteristic that one can name as 'belonging' to one sex can be found in some members of the 'opposite' sex. Some women, for example, have beards, and some men have been known to lactate when they have had babies who could not be fed otherwise. There are people with XY chromosomes who are androgen-insensitive and develop a vagina and a clitoris, and there are people with XX chromosomes who develop male genitalia. There are people who begin life as females and develop male genitalia around puberty (Crapo, 1985). There are people with micropenises and there are people who are born with a mixture of genitals and some with both sets complete. 'Male' hormones are produced in the female adrenal gland, and the brains of both men and women respond to male hormones only after they have been converted into female hormones.

The idea of man and woman as bipolar opposites has no more basis in physiology than the conceptual division of the world into stupid and intelligent people, or short and tall people, or beautiful and ugly people. The language suggests two discrete categories, into which all individuals can be made to fit, but simple inspection of these categories shows that they are a conceptual shorthand rather than an adequate way of dividing people into genuine bipolar camps. The words are bipolar, the people are not.

Haug (1987) describes some of the extreme trauma and anxiety experienced by many women who find they do not 'fit' the idea of the female body; and Connell, Radican and Martin (1987) discuss the problems many men experience in trying to achieve the ideals of hegemonic masculinity. The extreme difficulties that are encountered in the area of competitive sport in deciding absolutely the sex of the competitors provide a further illustration. Women who have all the physical attributes of women but who have some presence of Y chromosomes have been excluded from women's competitions on the basis that they are *not women*—though of course it is not concluded from this that they *are* men. Kessler and McKenna say of this kind of muddle that 'the biologists' criteria for gender become nonsensical when, in an attempt to be "fair", they are applied to everyday life' (1978:54).

When a child is born, it is usually the presence or absence of a penis that dictates whether it is assigned to the category male or female. But children who don't have penises do sometimes have internal male reproductive organs and XY chromosomes. Because females are defined in terms of lack of a penis rather than presence of a vagina and ovaries, it is quite common for children who are known to be genetically male to be raised as female. Rogers (1988) cites the case of male identical twin who lost his penis in an accident during circumcision. His parents decided to raise him as a girl and he grew up physically and socially quite different from the identical twin raised as a boy. He was thus genetically, hormonally and to some extent genitally a male, but socially and physically female. There are many other cases, such as children whose male genitals do not develop until adolescence and who, until the point where they become visibly genitally male, happily take up their lives as girls.

Kessler and McKenna cite research which shows that when children are 'mis-assigned' at birth (for example, the doctors decide on the basis of the absence of external male genitalia that the child is female but later discover the presence of a Y chromosome or internal male genitalia), reassignment can cause severe emotional disturbance after the age of eighteen months or two years. In other words a child who can be said to be biologically male, but has taken himself up socially as female, is not at all impressed with having to switch when he is just in the process of taking on as his own the knowledge of opposite sexes and in constituting his identity on the basis of this understanding. If biology were as important as it has been made out to be in shaping our social selves, these children should all experience relief at being reassigned, but this is far from the case.

There is no reliable evidence that 'male' behaviour follows from having male genitals, hormones or genes, or that 'female' behaviour follows from having female genitals, hormones or genes (Rogers, 1975, 1981, 1988). Rogers has shown how the biologists who have attempted to prove that brain function and social behaviour follow from male hormones or male genes have done so on the most unbelievably flimsy evidence and on the basis of quite fallacious arguments. The 'proof' that male hormones lead to a preference for career over domesticity, for example, was based on an experiment with males who were presumed to have greater or lesser amounts of androgen on the basis of their observable physique. Bigger, stronger males were seen to be more interested in pursuing their own interests (such as career) more vigorously than smaller, weaker males, and it was concluded from this that *all* males (who have more androgen than females) are therefore 'naturally' more oriented to careers than females. To 'prove' something about females by studying the differences between males does not seem to have struck these researches as odd. Nor does it seem to have occurred to them that there could be social factors involved in such differences (such as that bigger, stronger males are more used to having their own interests served). As Rogers points out, each of the biologists' findings can just as adequately be explained in terms of environment, or an interaction between environment and physiology. She claims it is quite premature for biologists to argue from behavioural sex differences to biological causes, since the evidence for this link is simply not there. It is not possible at this point in time to prove that we are simply biologically or socially determined; rather, Rogers suggests a subtle intertwining of physiology and environment which at this stage biologists still cannot tease apart.

The perception of that which is biologically male as opposite to that which is female can also be seen as an imposition of the social equation male=power/action, female=passivity/powerlessness. An excellent example of this is the way in which ovaries and sperm are unreflectively perceived by biologists. The ovary is usually described as passive and the sperm as active, which is a serious misconstruction of what actually happens when they unite—the ovary putting out a sticky substance which can be said to catch the sperm. Male and female genitals, too, are generally regarded as unproblematically 'opposite'—one active and projectile, the other inactive and receptive. And it is true that most people experience them that way since that is the way they are constituted through our discursive practices. But men and women can constitute their sexual being differently if they have access to different discursive practices. If one ceases to take for

10

granted the rule of opposition and difference, even genitals can be seen as remarkable for their similarity rather than their difference. The foreskin and/or the testicles can be seen as essentially similar to the labia, the penis has similarities to the clitoris, and the pubic hair is the same. There is no physiological reason for the male to be the dominant sexual partner, the one who controls the sex act. As Connell points out, it is not

> biologically decreed, by the architecture of the genitals, that Man must thrust and Woman lie still. (Though that is a belief on which a great tower of sub-Freudian bullshit has been erected, even by otherwise perceptive psychoanalysts.) This too is constructed, as a relation, in a practice of sexual encounter that begins with erection and ends with ejaculation, and in which woman's pleasure is marginal to what the man does, or is assumed to be guaranteed by powerful ejaculation. In eroticism focussed on the penis and on penetration, passive or gentle contact is likely to be dispensed with or hurried through, for fear of losing the erection, failing; and the man may be quite unable to come to climax except when moving, thrusting. (Connell, 1983:24)

Different discursive practices can construct the act quite differently, though the discursive practices that hold women into sexual passivity are extraordinarily powerful. The number of derogatory terms that are used to describe sexually active or dominant women and the actions that follow on those labellings are an essential element of those practices.

One of the most fascinating findings of recent biological research is that hormones are to some extent produced by gendered activity, rather than the other way round, Aggressive male interludes, for example, produce increased androgen, and periods of non-aggression a reduction in androgen (Kessler and McKenna, 1978; Rose et al., 1972; Sayers, 1986). The implication of this finding is that those people who do achieve themselves as a 'polar' male or female may well do so, at least in part, as a result of behaving in those ways that increase male or female hormones and thus accentuate their male or female physiology. Equally, those of us who are interested in positioning ourselves in ways that are traditionally reserved for the 'opposite' sex may also experience physiological shifts as a result of doing so. Girls who engage in high levels of physical fitness training, for example, sometimes cease to menstruate, and, as mentioned above, men have been known to lactate when engaging in high levels of nurturing.

This kind of evidence makes some non-feminists very anxious, and can in fact be taken as an argument to compel boys to behave like boys and girls like girls. Crapo (1985), in his discussion of some of these findings, barely conceals the note of hysterical panic that he feels as he imagines the end of the human species if we don't succeed in maintaining the difference and opposition between males and females. This panic is fascinating given the multiple and ingenious ways that different species have found to reproduce themselves in the absence of opposite and separate males and females. Our continuation does not depend on maintaining the opposition, though the idea that it does is a powerful piece of discourse for persuading people to continue positioning themselves as if the opposition and difference were not only natural but a morally binding obligation.

The critical distinction that we need to make is between male and female reproductive capacity and the masculine and feminine subject positionings that have usually been made available on the basis of that reproductive capacity. Male or female reproductive capacity does not have any *necessary* implication for the subjectivity or subject positionings that any individual can take up.

An assumption of poststructuralist theory is that maleness and femaleness do not have to be discursively structured in the way that they currently are. Genitals do not have to be linked to feminine or masculine subjectivities unless we constitute them that way. Children can take up a range of both masculine and feminine positionings if they have access to discourse that renders that non-problematic. Within poststructuralist theory the individual is no longer seen as a unitary, unproblematically sexed being, but rather as a shifting nexus of possiblities. In a world not polarised around a female—male dualism, these possibilities would not be limited by one's reproductive sexual capacity, but would be linked instead to the range of potential positionings each individual person was capable of or interested in taking up.

The process of positioning oneself as male or female

The position that I will explore in this book is that sex and gender are at one and the same time elements of the social structure, and something created by individuals and within individuals as they learn the discursive practices through which that social structure is created and maintained. Social structure is not separate from the individuals who make it up. It is not a 'thing' that can be imposed on individuals. It nevertheless has material force. Individuals cannot float free from social structure. They can choose to act on and transform structures, but structures must always be recognised as constraining individual and social action:

> ... practice, while presupposing structure ... is always responding to a *situation*. Practice is the transformation of that situation in a particular direction. To describe structure is to specify what it is in a particular situation that constrains the play of practice. Since the consequence of practice is a transformed situation which is the object of new practice, 'structure' specifies the way practice (over time) constrains practice.

12

> Since human action involves free invention ... can human knowledge is reflexive, practice can be turned against what constrains it; so structure can deliberately be the object of practice. But practice cannot escape structure, cannot float free from its circumstances ... It is always obliged to reckon with the constraints that are the precipitate of history.
> (Connell, 1987:95)

The polarised social structure, created through a multitude of different discursive practices, is something individuals can attempt to change through a refusal of certain discursive practices or elements of those practices, and by practising new and different forms of discourse. At the same time it is important to recognise that individuals are constrained by existing structures and practices. These are not simply an external constraint (or potentiation), they provide the conceptual framework, the psychic patterns, the emotions through which individuals position themselves as male or female and through with they privately experience themselves in relation to the social world. As well, they provide the vehicle through which others will recognise that positioning as legitimate, as meaningful, as providing the right to claim personhöod. The development and practice of new forms of discourse, then, is not a simple matter of choice, but involves grappling with both subjective and social/structural constraints.

Masculinity and femininity are not inherent properties of individuals, then, they are inherent or structural properties of our society: that is, they both condition and arise from social action. Each of us, as members of society, takes on board as our own the 'knowledge' of sex and of gender as they are socially constituted. As children learn the discursive practices of their society, they learn to position themselves correctly as male or female, since that is what is required of them to have a recognisable identity within the existing social order (Davies, 1987). Not to do so, in fact to resist, is to be perceived as a social failure (Haug, 1987; Walkerdine and Lucey, 1989). Positioning oneself as male or female is done through the discursive practices and through the subject positionings which are available within those practices, in much the same way and through the same practices that the positioning of 'child' and 'adult' are made available.

Take, for example, a situation in which I, as adult, say to you, as child, 'Good girl'. The major import of this is not that *I* choose to reward *you* for being a particular kind of girl and thus press you into a particular social mould, but that my use of the particular category 'good girl' in this particular situation creates and sustains both the gendered and the adultist elements of the social structure. By using a particular linguistic form I engage in the discursive practice which constitutes you as child, me as adult and your behaviour as praiseworthy and as relevant to your female genderedness. Through hearing me as speaking coherently in relation to the action you have just

13

performed, you see one of the ways in which the concepts of femaleness and virtue are linked by adults within the discursive practices of the society.

Children as well as adults are all members of a society which celebrates hegemonic (dominant, powerful) masculinity. Hegemonic masculinity is an *idea* of masculinity (as well as something practised by some men) that we generally refer to when we go along with those generalisations that make all men not only superior in terms of strength and power to women, but also *opposite* to women. Similarly, when we think of women who are the 'oppressed other' to such men we evoke a housebound mother of small children. All the rest of the men and women (which includes most women for most of their lives) somehow slip from our minds while we do this conceptual work to sustain the polarity. I will come back to this point in later chapters. The essential point at this stage is that no one individual stamps another individual in the mould of the society. Rather, the society provides, through its structures, its language and its interactive forms, possible ways of being, of thinking, of seeing (cf. Davies, 1983a; Garnica, 1979). Out of the multitude of conflicting and often contradictory possibilities, each person struggles to achieve themselves as a unitary, rational being whose existence is separate from others, and yet makes sense to those others. In learning the discursive practices we learn the categories, the relations between categories, and the fine conceptual and interactive detail with which to take up our personhood, and with which to interpret who we are in relation to others. Positioning oneself as person within the terms made available within a particular social order also creates and sustains that social order.

Positioning oneself as male or female is not just a conceptual process. It is also a *physical* process. Each child's body takes on the knowledge of maleness or femaleness through its practices. The most obvious, and apparently superficial, form of bodily practice that distinguishes male from female is dress and hairstyle. Many of the practices that are handed to children by adults, such as dress, serve to mark children such that their gender is emphasised and made a predominant feature of their appearance. Joanne, one of the children I encountered in the second stage of the study, tended to wear tracksuits all the time, at least during winter, these being much more suitable than dresses for the kind of activity she enjoyed. But she found that she was so constantly mistaken for a boy that she had to tie her hair up in a distinctively girlish top knot in order to avoid being so mistaken. She found people's inability to see that she was female distressing, presumably because she took it as a signal of her failure to be correctly gendered. She was, on several occasions, at pains to point out to me that she did own several dresses.

But the wearing of dresses is more than symbolic. It is an essential part of the process through which girls learn the meaning of being girls. Jackson comments:

> Sexual modesty is considered a specifically feminine virtue, so any signs of immodesty in girls are condemned most forcefully. In fact, girls are often so well schooled that they are even reluctant to reveal their bodies to other girls ... These problems are intensified by girls' clothing: if we teach children that it is indecent to reveal their underwear, and then proceed to dress half of them in skirts, we are placing that half at a distinct disadvantage. (1982:98−9)

Bruce comments on teachers finding 'many examples such as little girls being "punished" by the attitudes of others for behaviour such as hanging up side down from monkey bars and showing their knickers ...' (1985:52). Adams and Walkerdine (1986) found that dresses were central to boys' definitions of girls; and the Goldmans reported little boys being quite negative about the idea of being a girl on this basis: '7 year old boy: Boys wear trousers every day and girls usually wear dresses. People can pull them up and see their pants' (Goldman and Goldman, 1982:176). Thus dresses mark the femaleness of their wearers but they also act as part of the process whereby femaleness becomes inscribed in girls' bodies (see also Clark, forthcoming).

The process of bodily inscription works from the idea to the reality: what one is able to be is constrained by the idea of what one might be, and this is particularly the case in the division between males and females. Wex (1979) and Haug (1987), for example, have shown that girls are taught to sit in quite unnatural and submissive postures, with knees always together. Boys, in contrast, are free to sit more naturally with knees apart and they look dominant and assertive in doing so. Girls who sit in 'male' postures are not seen as assertive and dominant but as sexually provocative and 'available'. How we hold our bodies and how we interpret that holding depends on which gender we have been ascribed and what is counted as allowable within the frame of the gender one is taken to have (cf. also Herzberger and Tennen, 1985).

Similarly Adams and Walkerdine show that girls' and boys' violence is construed quite differently. They say that in boys violence 'can almost be turned into a positive quality, whereas "violent" girls are described in sexually pejorative terms: "bitch", "madam"' (Adams and Walkerdine, 1986:36).

There are a number of items of dress that are used by preschool children to mark their sex, such marking being a symbolic means of maintaining the sexes as clear distinct. Generally, skirts, ribbons, shawls, handbags, prams and dollies signify femaleness, and guns, trousers, waistcoats, coats, superhero capes and uniforms such as firefighters' uniforms signify maleness. These gendered symbols were closely associated by the children whom I studied with what they defined as male and female behaviour, so much so that they would cross-dress in order to achieve the behaviour they associated with the form of dress. When I first arrived at one of the preschools to carry out my observations there, I noticed several boys who were occasionally to be seen running around wearing a skirt from the dressing-up cupboard. On one occasion I saw a boy, whom I have called Geoffrey, in a black velvet skirt fighting furiously with another boy just near the home corner:

> Two boys start aggressive wrestling and punching. Geoffrey, the bigger of the two, seems to be getting the worst of it. He is dressed in a black velvet skirt. He starts to cry and shouts at the smaller boy, "You're yucky! You made me (unclear)!' He stands up and takes the skirt off angrily and throws it on the ground. He kicks the smaller boy, saying, "Now I've got more pants on!" The smaller boy starts to cry, no longer willing to fight back, he cowers away from Geoffrey's kicking. Once he has kicked him several times Geoffrey walks away, seemingly satisfied and no longer tearful. The black velvet skirt is left lying on the ground. (observation notes, St Michael's)

The skirts and trousers are more than superficial dressing. Not only can they constrict and sexualise girls, they can act as powerful signifiers of masculine and feminine ways of being. They appear to have a symbolic weight of perhaps equal if not greater significance for the children than the symbolic forms encoded in language.

There were also incidents in which girls dressed in 'male' clothes, or, rather, used male symbols to achieve a masculine form of action. These were less frequent. On one such occasion Catherine, a pretty girl who was always dressed in 'feminine' clothes and often to be found in the 'home corner', needed to get her dolly back from George who had stolen it from her:

> Catherine is dressing her dolly in the home corner. A small boy, John, who often plays with the girls in the home corner is 'ironing' the dolls' clothes. There is a new toy box in the home corner and Geoffrey comes in and jumps into it.
> CATHERINE: (to Geoffrey) You be the father.
> GEOFFREY: I'm not the father, I'm the fireman.
> JOHN: I'm ironing this jumper.
> CATHERINE: No, I'm just putting this doll here.
> (They cooperatively dress the doll.)
> GEORGE: (skipping into the room and singing) I'm going to get a dolly, dolly dolly, dolly dolly. Oh a toy box! A toy box! (He picks up a dolly.) A dolly for me. I want a dolly like that!
> CATHERINE: No it's my doll!
> (George goes off and bangs a cupboard door.)
> JOHN: We'd better ring your mum.
> (George comes back in, grabs Catherine's doll and runs off with it. She is on the verge of tears. John hands her the phone, then offers her dolls' clothes to put on another doll, attempting with the phone call and the suggestion of another doll to maintain their play, weaving in the theft to the storyline, so as not to disrupt it.)
> CATHERINE: No, that boy took it!

16

(John resumes ironing and Catherine wanders off, presumably to see if she can get her doll. She comes back without it.)

JOHN: Here you are, they're already ironed.

(Catherine, ignoring John, goes decisively to the dress-up cupboard and puts on a man's waistcoat. She tucks the waistcoat into the dress-up skirt that she already has on, and marches out. This time she returns victorious with the dolly under her arm. She immediately takes off the waistcoat and drops it on the floor. She is now very busy and happy.)

CATHERINE: Where are the stockings? (red tights for the doll)

(Sophie comes in with a dolly she is dressing. Catherine gets a flimsy white skirt out of the dress-up cupboard and puts it on as a cape, as if to emphasise her femininity. She and John go to the weighing machine which is just near the home corner, the doll apparently left behind in the home corner. They are preparing things for their dinner. The 'cape' is considerably hampering Catherine's movements.)

JOHN: You do yours and I'll do mine. Is yours burning?

CATHERINE: No. Now what's for dinner?

JOHN: Sausages. (The banksia cones that had been provided for play with the weighing machines make admirable sausages.)

CATHERINE: Right. I'll take off this skirt. (she removes the skirt recently put on as a cape)

(They proceed to have their dinner and Catherine to dress the dolly.) (video notes, St Michael's)

Thus, as we discursively position ourselves as male or female, it can be argued, our physical being will follow suit. The knowledge of oneself as male or female, encoded in one's body, makes possible, or precludes, certain forms of relationship with others and with the landscape. How one understands what one's body can or cannot do immediately affects the way one's body relates to the environment. That is, the idea of femaleness and the adoption of practices relevant to that idea has a material effect on the child's body. One's sex is thus *inscribed* in one's body through the activities associated with one's *ascribed* sex (cf. Gross, 1986a; Haug, 1987).

An excellent analysis of this difference in bodily inscription is undertaken by Young (1980). Young cites the work of Strauss on the different ways that very young boys and girls throw balls. Strauss says:

The girl of five does not make any use of lateral space. She does not stretch her arm sideward; she does not twist her trunk; she does not move her legs, which remain side by side. All she does in preparation for throwing is to lift her right arm forward to the horizontal and to bend the forearm backward in a pronate position ... The ball is released without force, speed or accurate aim ... A boy of the same age, when preparing to throw, stretches his right arm sideward and backward; supinates the forearm; twists, turns and bends his trunk; and moves his right foot backward. From this stance, he can support his throwing almost with the full strength of his total motorium ... The ball leaves the hand with considerable acceleration; it moves towards its goal in a long flat curve (Strauss, 1966:157–8).

17

Young analyses the difference between these two forms of throwing in terms of the 'inhibited intentionality' that comes with learning to see oneself primarily as the object of another's gaze, and the learned sense of fragility that comes with being female. She concludes that lack of practice is only one aspect of the problem:

> The modalities of feminine bodily existence are not merely privative, however, and thus their source is not merely lack of practice, though this is certainly an important element. There is a specific positive style of feminine body comportment and movement, which is learned as the girl comes to understand that she is a girl ... In assuming herself as a girl, she takes herself up as fragile ... The more a girl assumes her status as feminine, the more she takes herself to be fragile and immobile, and the more she actively enacts her own body inhibition ... At the root of these modalities ... is the fact that the woman lives her body as *object* as well as subject ... An essential part of the situation of being a woman is that of living the ever present possibility that one will be gazed upon as a mere body, as shape and flesh that presents itself as the potential object of another subject's intentions and manipulations, rather than as a living manifestation of action and intention. (Young, 1980:153–4)

As well, an attitude or understanding of oneself as male or female involves learning the *emotions* relevant to male and female subject positionings. For girls, particularly, this involves knowing what is desirable/attractive about oneself and how that attractiveness affects others. Closely related to that knowledge is a knowledge of one's place in the narrative structures in the culture—as child and as potential adult—as one who loves or hates in this or that way inside this or that narrative, or who is loved or hated in terms of those same narratives (cf. Cranny-Francis, 1988). The psychic organisation of fantasy and desire derives from the imaginary placement of oneself as male or female within the narrative structures as well as through one's experience of the subject positionings made available in interactions with others. The imagined self and the self made possible through interactions are closely woven together, each lending meaning to the other.

The *idea* of bipolar maleness—femaleness is something which itself has material force. This is evidenced by the continuing work each person engages in to achieve and sustain their gendered identity, and by the fact that when they fail to do so, they perceive themselves, and are perceived by others, as failing as an individual, rather than perceiving the linguistic structures in which the dualism is embedded as at fault. One of the ways in which the idea of bipolarity functions is to reduce the *actual diversity* (non-polarity) of individual behaviour to a bipolar model. This can involve ignoring or not seeing 'deviations' or actually managing to construe behaviour or categories of behaviour as bipolar, even though they would appear to lend themselves more readily to a non-polar perception. I suspect, for example, that the idea that it is women who engage in nurturing behaviour and who are involved in a network of caring, and men who are caught up in an ethic of individual rights (Gilligan, 1982) can function in two ways in terms of perceiving what it is that people actually do. The first is to highlight deviant behaviour—for example, men who engage in 'feminine' forms of caring are seen as engaging in exceptional and very large amounts of caring. The second is to make the behaviour more difficult to see—the man who engages in 'masculine' forms of caring, such as protecting someone weaker is not seen as having done any caring at all.

Several of the children with whom I worked in the first stage of the study showed a remarkable capacity to keep the idea of the dualism intact by ignoring individual deviations, or managing to construe those deviations as somehow fitting into the bipolar system. The following episode, for example, took place during a reading of the story *Jesse's Dream Skirt*. In this story Jesse has a dream that he has a beautiful multi-coloured skirt. In the morning his mother makes him the skirt out of her old dresses and he insists on wearing it to preschool. Jesse is teased by the others but the teacher persuades them that it is all right for Jesse to dress in this way. Chonny was very angry at the thought of a boy choosing to wear a skirt or a dress:

B.D.: Do you ever wear a dress?
CHONNY: (shakes head)
B.D.: What about Daddy? Does Daddy sometimes wrap himself up in a dress?
CHONNY: No. My mum.
B.D.: Your mum does. But sometimes doesn't Dad wrap himself around with a skirt? (pointing to picture of a man in a sarong, knowing that his father wore sarongs, but not using the word 'sarong', suspecting that it is not part of Chonny's vocabulary)
CHONNY: No.
B.D.: Doesn't he? (doubtful tone of voice)
CHONNY: Mans don't have some!
B.D.: Don't they? Well this boy does doesn't he? (pointing at Jesse) And these men here do, all these different men, a priest and this Greek person (pointing at pictures in the front of the book)
CHONNY: Um (unclear)
B.D.: This boy's dressing up in his mum's clothes.
CHONNY: Sometimes big girls do that.
B.D.: Big girls? Do boys ever try on their mother's dresses?
CHONNY: No.
B.D.: Well this boy does.
CHONNY: I don't either.
B.D.: Right.
CHONNY: I do have pants.
B.D.: Why don't boys try on dresses? Don't they think/
CHONNY: They don't have some. (said with finality)

Later, when I took him home, he burst out to his Malay father that I had read him this stupid story about a boy who wore a dress. Interestingly, his father had a friend visiting who was wearing a sarong, and thus looking very like the men pictured at the front of the book, but this cut no ice with Chonny. The fact that his father and his father's friend observably wore what could be called dresses needed to be ignored, or construed as not fitting into the category of 'dress' in order to maintain not only the symbolic boundaries of the categories male and female, but their exclusiveness from each other.

Another child, this time a Persian boy at one of the pre-schools I observed, also managed the same feat in relation to strength as a defining feature of males. He told me that because he was a boy he was stronger than girls, and gave as an example the fact that he helped his sister, who was weak, over puddles. Shortly afterwards one of the girls of the same age hitched herself up onto a fairly high window sill behind her in order to sit on it. Hamid made a feeble attempt to do the same thing then whinged for me to lift him up too, knowing that he did not have the strength and agility to match the girl's feat. Once up, however, he countinued in his domineering manner, utterly unshaken by this contrary evidence to his earlier assertion.

Each child must get its gender right, not only for itself to be seen as normal and acceptable within the terms of the culture, but it must get it right for others who will be interpreting themselves in relation to it as other. To the extent that it is a competent member of society, it can be seen to be competently constructing the gendered world, achieving the practices, the ways of knowing and of being that make sense within the narrative/interactive structures of the society it lives in. That achievement in turn is treated to a large extent as a *natural* expression of maleness or femaleness, such interpretations being aided by the association in our culture of the body with that which is natural.

Once having taken on the bodily, emotional and cognitive patterns which give substance to the dominance—subordinance forms of gender relations, it is difficult for individuals to imagine any alternative to that social structure. In turn, the apparent facticity of two opposite genders renders those behaviours, thoughts and emotions which are involved in stepping outside the dominant (male) and subordinate (female) patterns appear as incompetence, even immorality. The failure to be 'correctly' gendered is perceived as a moral blot on one's identity since that which is believed to be is, and generally takes on the weight of a moral imperative—there are, we believe, two opposite sexes, therefore that is the way the world *ought* to be.

2 Researching with children

The first stage of data-collection for this study evolved out of those early incidents described in the Introduction. I chose a variety of feminist stories and began intensive work with eight individual four- and five-year-old children. Many hours were spent with each child, over a period of one year, reading the stories that they selected from the range of stories I had found, and discussing what they thought of each story as we went. With five of the children we met in my office to record our talk. Sometimes we listened to the recorded talk and sometimes played with plasticine, creating and playing with the characters in the story. Usually after an hour or so we wandered up to the student cafeteria to have a drink along with something to eat and a chat about life in general, before resuming our work. The form of these pleasant mornings was dictated to a large extent by what the children wanted to do. They enjoyed these sessions very much, and always asked for further sessions. One child, Anika, commented that she enjoyed the work we were doing because she felt important, as if she were at a meeting like the ones that each of her parents went to. Three of the children did not live in Armidale and so the interviews with them took place in their own homes. Of necessity I conducted fewer sessions with these three than I did with the others. The eight children, whom I have called Anika, Gabrielle, Sebastian, Robbie, Mark, Leo, Katy and Chonny, ranged in age between four and a half and five and a half. None was at school yet, though all were currently attending pre-school. The first six had middle-class parents with professional backgrounds. Of these, Anika, Gabrielle, Mark and Leo all had mothers who worked at relatively high-status jobs, while Sebastian and Robbie had mothers with high educational attainment who believed that it was better for their children if they had mothers who did not go out to work. Katy and Chonny, in contrast, had mothers

21

with little education and with no ambitions to work, at least while their children were small. Katy's father was a tradesman and Chonny's father was a student. All of them, rather predictably, had fathers with higher educational and professional attainment than their mothers.

I was able to get to know each of these children well, with the exception of Chonny who had little or no experience of having stories read to him and so did not really have the required skills for participating in this stage of the research. His mother could not read and so the method he had learned of dealing with books was to look at the pictures and ask questions about them. He had no idea of listening to something being read in order to hear what the story is about, nor of gaining information from printed words in general. He was also used to having his little brother turn the pages at random and so had no idea of waiting for someone to finish telling what is to be told on any one page, or of moving sequentially through a book. As well, he chose different stories from the other children and refused to listen to what had become the popular stories with every-one else. The experience with Chonny, while frustrating, was a salutary one, because it drew my attention to the extent to which I had been taking very complex skills for granted in my work with the other children (see Steedman, 1985).

The second stage of data-collection, which took place over the second year of the study, involved visiting a number of the preschools and childcare centres in order to observe the way in which the things that children said related to their everyday activities. I chose four venues, two in Armidale, one in Sydney and one in Melbourne. The Sydney preschool catered for children from upper-middle-class families, and the Armidale preschool catered for children from all backgrounds but tended to be preferred by middle-class parents. The two childcare centres, one in Armidale and one in Melbourne, specifically catered for children of poorer parents, being well subsid-ised and caring for children for the full working week. This range was chosen to ensure that I did not fall into the trap of asserting a limited middle-class or rural version of childhood and of gender relations. During the final stages of writing this book I was able to discuss my findings with people working with small children in the United States and in England, and was able to establish that what I have found in Australia is comparable to what I would have found in these countries had I conducted the research there.

The greatest amount of time was spent at St Michael's, Armidale, observing the children, reading them stories, and audio- and video-recording their play. This took place two days a week over a period of three months. In each of the other three venues I spent one full week collecting data. At Moore St this involved video-taping, but at Lothlorien and Inner City I relied on audio-recordings. The rest of my time during that year was spent transcribing and analysing the rich data that I had on my video- and audio-recordings.

A note on class and race

To the extent that this study draws on children's responses to stories in books, it is a study of children located in literate rather than oral cultures. As well, to the extent that the stories are Western in their characters and content, they cannot be assumed to map onto the storylines of non-Western cultures. Although there were some non-Western children included in the study, I was not able to spend enough time with them to be able to come up with any reasonable comparative data. Other studies could be devised to explore the experience of children in other cultures, but would need to be developed on the basis of an understanding of the narrative structures in those cultures. While I ensured in the second stage of the study that I had a range of children from different class and ethnic backgrounds, I have not treated class and race as 'variables', nor as categories into which people can be placed. Class and race, if they can be used at all, should simply be used as aids in mapping the range of discursive practices that children have available to them. Because class and race are not unitary, nor determining features of persons, but labels that we use to group people with, I have not divided and compared the children according to these categories, though in Chapter 6 I have given some information on parental class background insofar as it appears to bear an interesting relation to some of the discursive practices that the children engage in.

St Michael's Preschool

St Michael's is the first of the rural preschools. The first impression one has here is of sunshine, space, green fields and children running, climbing and playing. Inside and outside merge into one another, the inside spaces being filled with light and air and the doors always open. The building is a modified cottage with many of the inner walls removed, windows added and ramps built up to the front door. The spacious, grassy outside playing area has a multitude of well-kept equipment for climbing, jumping, sliding, swinging, digging, painting, hammering and hiding. Inside, there is one room for each of the following activities: painting, playing house, craft-work, building blocks and looking at books. The 'home corner' is a particularly fascinating place, being very well equipped and maintained, and where a great deal of domestic fantasy is played out. The staff members appear relaxed, and spend time chatting to parents and children. Most of their time is spent in loose supervision, the children being almost entirely free to choose their activities.

23

Occasionally groups of children are drawn together for stories, or for music, but involvement is not compulsory. All children gather together at morning teatime, sitting out in the sun to eat fruit and drink fruit juice. The teachers' explicit philosophy is humanistic, that is, that children should learn to be autonomous and that the teacher's task is to teach them the physical and interpersonal skills they need to be so. However, they generally intervene in the children's play only when the children's own strategies fail them and they come to the teacher for help.

Moore St Children's Centre

Moore St is also a rural centre, but the children are generally from poorer families and tend to stay all day at the centre rather than coming in for several mornings or afternoons as they do at St Michael's. The play inside and out is much more controlled by the teachers and there is not a great deal of fantasy play to be observed. Inside and outside are strongly demarcated, and the children are organised for inside and outside play at times decided by the teachers. There was not as much opportunity for me to talk to the children because of this high level of organisation. The playing area does not have the rich abundance of St Michael's, the sandpit, swings and climbing frame providing the major entertainment. The inside area is one large room with book shelves as dividers. There are some dolls but no 'home corner' and none of the usual equipment one associates with 'home corners'. Hot lunches are provided by the centre and the teachers sit down formally at tables with the children and eat with them. The teachers' interactions with the children seemed to be based on traditional assumptions about adult–child relations, that is, their task was to care for them physically, to order their days and to teach them acceptable ways of being (such as how to cooperate, take turns and settle differences).

Lothlorien Preschool

Lothlorien Preschool is part of a progressive private primary school. Located in an elite city suburb, the school is housed in an old but very attractive two-storey house. Both the outside and inside playing areas have a multitude of nooks and crannies where children can escape from adult attention altogether. Some activites are organised by adults (such as painting, and cutting and pasting), but the children are free to wander where they choose, to eat their packed lunches when they choose, or to join in adult organised activities when it suits them. The atmosphere is relaxed and friendly with a studied inattention to dirt and noise. The 'home corner' is a neglected, dusty area with a couple of dolls lying on the floor. These did not

24

appear to have been moved during the entire week I was there. The noise level was so high at times when I was attempting to talk to the children that recording was almost impossible. Even when we searched for a quiet place there was none to be found. One of the major ideals of the staff was that the boundaries between adults and children should be broken down: children should take responsibility for their own learning and be treated with the kind of respect that is normally accorded only to adults. This was not accompanied, however, by any demand that the children behave like adults—it was quite the reverse. The belief in autonomy was accompanied by a belief that children should be free to 'be themselves'. This dual belief placed a high level of stress on the teachers.

Inner City Children's Centre

Inner City is a modern day-care centre for babies through to four- and five-year-olds. The first impression is of order, well-designed buildings, caring staff. The adults are clearly separate from the children—a separate category of persons, displaying the kind of benevolent, intimate authority one usually associates with parenting. The activities are ordered according to a fixed schedule as at Moore St, but the children have a lot of time in which they are free to choose activities. Therefore they had more freedom to talk to me and to their teachers than the children at Moore St. The teachers knew each individual child well. There was much less outside space than at any of the other places I observed and so there was not as much running around—activities were much more tightly con-strained in terms of movements and play than in the other more spacious centres. The children were under a teacher's eye at all times. As at Moore St there were a number of children from non-Anglo-Australian backgrounds whose parents worked in unskilled and poorly paid jobs.

The research question

In talking with, observing and playing with these children, my central problem was to understand how the male—female duality is established and maintained. I wanted to know what being male or female actually meant to them in terms of the conceptual frameworks they used to make sense of being male or female, and in terms of the way their concepts were translated into practical activity in the everyday world. I wanted to know, as well, how it is that the majority of children adopt traditional male and female patterns of behaviour when this is not what many of their parents say they want. I wanted to know how the boundaries between male and female are created and maintained despite the extent of actual similarities between individual males and females, particularly amongst preschool children.

I will show—through my conversations with, my observations of and my interactions with the children of my study—how bipolar maleness and femaleness is learned, struggled with and adopted. The children's fantasies as evidenced in their play and in their responses to the feminist stories will be analysed to find the meanings of maleness and femaleness for them, and to search out ways of moving beyond the current dualism that binds males and females into these limited and oppositional positions.

I chose children of this age because they have moved outside the family circle into the more public world of preschool and thus had the experience of elaborating their identities in a context wider than their immediate family circle. The contrasts and contradictions they have inevitably met in this extension of their interpersonal world meant that they had quite a lot to say about being male and female.

The first stage of data-collection

In talking to the children during the first stage of data-collection, what I got was, to a certain extent, a rational 'cleaned-up' version of their reality. The process of articulating one's experience does essentially require this kind of cleaning up, insofar as language itself imposes a particular kind of order—the available words and orderings of words admitting only a certain range of possible meanings, one of which must be selected and others for the moment allowed to fall by the wayside. What one does with words is to make an event or experience understandable, something that can be told, something that draws on known concepts to order the myriad events around one. This involves, amongst other things, removing the contradictory elements of experience, choosing a focus that allows a clear and consistent storyline to emerge. But because the children had not yet learned to define all contradictions as non-allowable, the contradictions they experienced were sometimes not removed from their talk. This aspect of children's talk makes it closer to their experience than much adult talk, but it also makes it difficult for adults who have learned to define reality as non-contradictory to hear what the children are saying as making sense.

Another aspect of their talk is its *emergent* quality, like the building of sandpits by the preschool children that Silvers observed (1979). That is, the children do not launch into the conversation with the express purpose of giving me a preconceived theory of gender relations any more than Silvers' children set out to build a particular kind of castle. Just as Silvers' children responded to the condition of the sand and events that occurred during the building of the castle to allow a castle to emerge from their activity, so the children in this study give explanations of their thinking as this is asked for and in relation to the unfolding story.

Stories are one of the primary means that adults use to make available to children the kind of rational ordering of the social world that they themselves believe in. Children's stories use many of the dualisms of Western thought to present this ordered world. They show this is how the world is, or ought to be. This is how people are. There are goodies and baddies, males and females, adults and children. Baddies are punished—or triumph and become goodies. In stories there is order, there is a *place* for everyone who appears in the story, and this order is usually a moral order (Zipes, 1982).

The children's conversations in relation to the stories I read them were often about the moral order—about the way the world is or ought to be. Many of the feminist elements in the stories I read them, they saw as straightforwardly wrong. Or else they used elements of the traditional moral order to understand and explain the apparent aberrations of the characters in the stories. Princess Elizabeth in *The Paper Bag Princess* was often seen as bad once she had stepped out of her female place. There was no place in the narrative structure, as many of the children understood it, for a feminist hero.

The following conversation, which occurred with Robbie in relation to *Oliver Button is a Sissy*, illustrates this attention to the moral order. *Oliver Button is a Sissy* is a story in which larger boys give Oliver a really hard time because he does not behave how boys are 'supposed' to behave. Robbie does not censor the apparently contradictory elements of his explanation. He simply tells the world as he knows it, as that knowing is made relevant by my questions:

1 B.D.: So why doesn't Oliver Button like to play 'boys' games'?
2 ROBBIE: Because he likes girls' things.
3 B.D.: Because he likes girls' things. Mmm. (reads about Oliver Button going to dancing school) So all the others are little girls, aren't they (looking at picture)
4 ROBBIE: That's wrong.
5 B.D: It's wrong is it? So you wouldn't want Oliver to go? If you were Oliver and you hated all the boy's things and you wanted to do girl's things, would you want to go to dancing school?
6 ROBBIE: No.
7 B.D.: (reads about boys teasing Oliver) So what sort of boys are they?
8 Robbie: Big, they/
9 B.D.: Big boys, and should they say that to Oliver Button?
10 ROBBIE: Yes.
11 B.D.: They should? (surprised) . . . (reads about boys writing 'Oliver Button is a Sissy' on the school wall) How does Oliver feel?
12 ROBBIE: Sad.
13 B.D.: He's very sad isn't he? So should the boys have written that on the wall?

27

14 ROBBIE: (nods)
15 B.D.:   They should? (surprised) why should they have written that on the wall?
16 ROBBIE: Because he, because he's a sissy doing tap dancing.
17 B.D.:   (reads about Oliver practising his dancing) So why do you suppose he keeps going even though everybody keeps giving him a hard time?
18 ROBBIE: Because he just wants to.
19 B.D.:   He just wants to and should you keep doing what you want to do even though everyone keeps giving you a hard time?
20 ROBBIE: (nods)
21 B.D.:   Uh huh. (reads story) So his dad doesn't mind any more does he, that he's a tap dancer. Why do you suppose that is?
22 ROBBIE: Because he was good on stage.
23 B.D.:   Uh huh. So if you keep doing something that you're not supposed to do if you're a boy and you get to be good at it then it's quite alright?
24 ROBBIE: (nods)
25 B.D.:   Uh huh.

From an adult perspective some of the questions that arise in this conversation are: how can Robbie think it both right to tease someone who is deviating *and* right for a person to do what they want to do? And how can it be that he knows how Oliver feels and yet still believes that the teasing should go ahead? Within a traditional model of adult–child relations, Robbie would be assumed not to know what he is talking about, and in need of being taught how to think rationally (that is, as adults believe they should and hope they do). Assuming, however, that Robbie does know what he is talking about, and listening carefully to that talk in the context of the other children's talk and activity, it is possible to hear Robbie as correctly interpreting two contradictory aspects of the discourse that is available to him.

Through his class membership in particular, but also through his membership in the category of males, he has learned a discourse which condones and even celebrates the rights of the individual (cf. Gilligan, 1982). Through his membership in the collective of all gendered beings, however, he has learned to see gender as publicly owned and as requiring collective activity to maintain the gendered social order. Robbie believes it is 'wrong' for Oliver to go to the dancing school (4). Whether he liked dancing or not, whether he hated boy's things or not, the fact remains that he had got it wrong. Teasing is important in maintaining the social fabric, the categories male and female, which Oliver is clearly putting under threat (5–10). At the same time Robbie believed that Oliver's wish as an individual to break the rules justified his continuation at dancing school (17–20) and that his success legitimated his deviation.

Thus individuals *can* deviate, but their deviation will give rise to *category-maintenance work* around the gender boundaries. This category-maintenance work is aimed partly at letting the 'deviants' know they've got it wrong—teasing is often enough to pull someone back into line—but primarily it is aimed at maintaining the category as a meaningful category in the face of the individual deviation which is threatening it.

What adults often see is incomprehensible nastiness on the part of small children is in fact category-maintenance work which is necessary to the extent that competent social membership presumes gender, that is, gender that is defined in terms of male and female as opposite and antithetical. The category-maintenance work is important to the people who are doing it, since it is through such maintenance work that they clarify their own social competence—I am male, the way you are behaving is not how males behave. I may feel sorry for you, I may even have a fascination with the way you are doing your masculinity, but my aggression is essential in defining what you do as a transgression and clarifying for myself that I have got it right. One might even say that the 'deviants' are necessary for making stronger boundaries. Thus deviation does not change the category, but is used as an opportunity to shore the category up (cf. Connell et al., 1987).

There is a general assumption made in relation to children, usually within a traditional framework of adult—child relations, that contradictions are somehow bad for children, that we should be presenting them with a non-contradictory world. I would argue in relation to this that there is no such thing as a non-contradictory world since the world is not actually a unitary linear place, though we attempt to behave as if it is. Moreover, it can be argued that contradictions, when they are recognised as such, provide the creative cutting edge with which individual identities are formed (Haug, 1987). Within Western logic, opposites cannot both be true. That which is true cannot also be false, or the opposite of that which is true cannot also be true. But the diversity of human experience is filled with contradictory truths, since each of the multiple subject positionings we take up does not have the same set of coordinates as the last. Those positioned as female, in particular, have learned in reading stories for example, both to position themselves as male hero and to see themselves also positioned as other, as outside male reality. That is, they have been both viewer and viewed, insider and outsider (cf. Schweickart, 1986). Learning to be both and to make that opposition unproblematic is the way many girls have coped with their educational experiences.

In the first stage of the data-collection, the children had the opportunity to display through their talk their knowledge of the gendered world, their knowledge of the world as it is ordered through stories *and* to display, through their talk as well as their actions, their knowledge of interactions with adults, in this case the researcher.

The way in which I interacted with the children in this first stage was probably in many ways typical of any adult interacting with a child. There are undoubtedly assumptions I made about my rights as adult—for example, that the children speak politely to me— that I was not particularly aware of at the time. However, my intention was that their status as *children* not dictate my style of interacting with them, and that I accord them the same respect, civility and trust that I would accord an adult. Their interest in and enthusiasm about exploring their own understandings of gender relations were essential for the project to go ahead and that interest and enthusiasm was not something that I could require of them. Occasionally I found that their assumptions about how adult—child relations are organised were different from my own and I requested that they be ordered in the way I wanted them. For example, when I was driving Anika in my car she expected me to open the car door for her and to fasten her seat belt. I had to explain to her that I found that kind of helplessness hard to take and I suggested that she learn how to do these things—which she did instantly and with pleasure. On other occasions I was more tolerant, especially with Chonny, since the gap between what he understood about the ways one ought to be in the world and what I understood seemed too vast to close. As he smeared food all over the books and belligerently turned the pages, not heeding my request that he listen to the words, telling me that my interpretations of the pictures were wrong, I kept my cool by walking around the room several times and then sitting down to try again.

The children did not always have the words to 'tell' their experience. To this extent, some of their experiences could be described as pre-linguistic. That is, their experience is something they have not attended to consciously, or something that they have not spent time thinking about, or it may be so out of keeping with the order of the world as they understand it that they do not know what sense to make of it. Whenever the children did not know how to answer my questions they said so, or they changed the topic or suggested we get on with the story. They did not display any sense of obligation to tell me what I wanted to hear—in fact it was quite the reverse—I did not disguise my dismay over many of their interpretations and yet this did not change those responses one jot. I simply became another person who needed to have the way the world really is explained to her.

Despite the children's greater tolerance of contradiction, they often did attend only to one aspect of their experience rather than another, perhaps not seeing other aspects as relevant, or not remembering them at the time of formulating their response. Such failure to remember perfectly illustrates the complexity of the social world. In order to 'make sense' the complexity is reduced, one portion of one's experience or one subject positioning is recalled and is used to represent the whole. This process became evident to me on a few occasions.

The first occasion followed a reading of *Benjamin and Tulip* with Gabrielle. Benjamin is a very good and kind little boy who is forever being given a very hard time by a girl in the neighbourhood called Tulip. To make matters worse, Aunt Fern, who looks after Benjamin, blames Benjamin for everything and constantly asserts that Tulip is a sweet little thing. In discussing the story, Gabrielle maintained that Aunt Fern was in the right. It was as if it was unthinkable that an adult, at least in the moral framework of a story, could be wrong. On the way home in the car I challenged her with this, asking her whether her mother was ever in the wrong. She said yes, she was, gave me an example and told me how mad she got with her mother when this happened. I asked her why she hadn't used this knowledge when we were discussing Aunt Fern, and she said she hadn't thought of it. Although the story in my perception had been attempting actively to challenge the idea that adults are always right, this was not what Gabrielle heard. The expectation she was bringing to the story was that the moral order, in which adults are always right, would be reiterated.

A second occasion, this time with Anika, occurred after a reading of *The Princess and the Dragon*. This is the story of a bad princess who is unhappy being a princess and a sweet dragon who is unhappy being a dragon. The two swap places and are very happy. During the reading Anika said she preferred the sweet dragon who had become the princess and would like to be like her. I said this surprised me greatly because I could see no resemblance between her and the sugar-sweet dragon, but that there was a great deal of similarity between her and the fun-loving rough, tough princess. She denied this categorically. Her *desire* was to be the kind of child adults like. Though she might behave like the rough, tough princess, the sweet dragon represented what she knew was attractive to adults, and her desire to be attractive to some extent contradicted and ran counter to the ways she observably enjoyed being. Adults are clearly powerful others in developing patterns of desire and an understanding of the way one *ought* to be in the adult moral order. When I took Anika home she went and got some plasticine and put dobs of it on her face to look like the dirty princess in the story and ran around wildly, giggling with delight, a joke which she and I enjoyed, but which did not impress her mother.

On the other hand, one of the advantages of using the fantasies in the stories as the basis of our talk was that we maximised the opportunity to talk about things that the children may only have apprehended intuitively before. No doubt they could not have told me, if I had asked them directly, that they approve of women who are active agents in the world, or whether they saw such women as whores or witches who should learn their place; or that while they believed in romantic mythology of male—female relations, they nonetheless believed that women should have choices, and so on. Indeed, if I had attempted such questions I would have been regarded as a typical adult whose questions are essentially her own problem. But through the medium of the stories we were able to explore these generally unarticulated and contradictory ways of seeing and of being, and the children were able to provide those insights which would probably not have been available otherwise.

The second stage of data-collection

The range of methods of data-collection in this second stage allowed a different kind of insight into the children's perception of gender. Their fantasy play, because it involved the construction of narratives, provided an important adjunct to my understanding of their responses to the stories that I read them. For this reason I spent a great deal of my time in the 'home corner' at St Michael's and outside where many of the boys located their fantasy play. These were, unfortunately, much more difficult to observe discreetly since they generally involved multiple locations and a great deal of running from one location to the other.

The second stage of the research did not generally allow the same depth of relationship with each child, though there were two children at St Michael's, Joanne and George, who found the subject positionings available to the other sex highly desirable and with whom I spent many hours. They each became important catalysts in my thinking.

Gaining access

Unlike the children in the first stage, the children in the second stage had no choice about whether I was there, though they had a great deal more choice about whether they talked to me. In the first stage of the study there was a personal agreement prior to the event negotiated through the parents or more usually directly with the child, which meant that in agreeing to participate each child already had a commitment to talking to me. In the preschools and childcare centres I was there because the teachers approved of my presence and were interested in what I was going to do. I thus, ironically, had much less power in this situation to negotiate access to the children's talk and their play. The children did not necessarily want an adult hanging around them, nor did they know what sort of an adult I was. On several occasions the children asserted their right to be left alone. When I first asked Brigitta and Tegan, at Lothlorien, for example, whether they would like me to read them a story, they simply said 'no' and then proceeded to ignore me. I was shocked at their rudeness but respected their ability to make such choices. (I later discovered that story-telling at Lothlorien was one aspect of the day that was highly formal, conservative and boring. If Brigitta and Tegan had interpreted me to be suggesting such an event it is not at all surprising that they said no.) Sharon and Natasha and Marilla told me, when I first arrived at Inner City, that my name was 'shut up'. This was the fourth of my studies and by then I was used to the children's assumption of power in the preschool setting. I played along with their strategy for keeping me in my place, clapping my hand over my mouth in a humorous gesture after I had 'accidentally' spoken to one of the teachers who was coming over to tell the girls not to be rude, thus indicating that I knew that they meant that I shouldn't speak and at the same time that I was not one of the teachers:

NATASHA: (to me) Kaka, your name's kaka. (giggling)
SHARON: Your name's kaka, poo, wee wee.
MARILLA: What's her name?
NATASHA: Kaka wee wee. That's what your name is isn't it?
SHARON: Yes.
B.D.: What a horrible name.
NATASHA: It's a beautiful name.
MARILLA: Your name is Bibi. (laughter)
NATASHA: Shut up.
SHARON: You have to be quiet if your name is shut up.
B.D.: It's all right. (to the teacher) Oops, I just said something! (I clap my hand over my mouth)
NATASHA: Shut up! (following some conversation) Not you because your name is shut up.
B.D.: Right.
NATASHA: You talked one more time and now you shut up.
NATASHA: (later) Your name is talking.
(and so I was allowed into the conversation)

(audio transcript, Inner City)

In contrast, the way that children behaved with their parents was generally organised on the basis of a presumed powerlessness and helplessness such as that displayed by the boys in the yellow rain-coats. But many of the children were markedly agentic in the playg-round—they were powerful, aware and competent negotiators, and adults (with all of their power to control the way things are done) were necessarily marginalised by these children in their play. To the extent that children do this, there is much that goes on between children that adults often do not know about and to which it is difficult for any researcher to gain access except as a non-participating bystander, as I was in the yellow raincoat episode. Particularly where children are given freedom, and encouraged to act as autonomous beings as they were at St Michael's and Lothlorien, the adult world is made quite separate by the children and called on only as an ordering device when the childhood world gets unmanageable. For the most part the children operated with each other in these settings as if the teachers didn't exist, unless the teachers approached them or unless they needed them. This was not so marked at either of the childcare centres where the adults were always in close proximity and had to be accommodated as an ever-present part of the landscape. Activities and conversations about things adults might disapprove of had to be conducted more discreetly here, though they could rely to a certain extent on the fact that the adults would not actively listen and attend to their meanings unless conversation was specifically directed at them. At St Michael's and Lothlorien the only children who made adults relevant in their play were those who had not yet formed relationships with other children and so needed teachers as interactive stopgap others, something like a contingency friend. When things got tough out in the playground, a frequent strategy was to place oneself in the vicinity of an adult so that the aggressor's activity could be held in check, though without the victim having to admit that she/he was actually seeking help. Only children who had not yet figured how to cope in the playground would actually call directly on the teacher. This could lead to a scathing response such as Simon received in the following episode:

SIMON: Teacher said to play (the boys ignore him) . . . Teacher! Teacher! Teacher!
TONY: How could the teacher get all of us with the one of her?

It was this children's world, apparently not ordered by adults, that I particularly sought access to in the second stage.

One of the most immediately obvious features of the children's world is how awful it is not to have a friend or group of friends to play with. Some children worked hard to prevent their parents from leaving (usually by producing an exaggerated form of helplessness) until one of their friends appeared.

The 'correct' behaviour when you want to play with someone can be very complicated and require a high level of interpersonal competence. As Corsaro (1979) has demonstrated, knowing how an ongoing game works, and knowing how to produce, at the appropriate moment, dialogue relevant to that game, is highly important for access to group play. In other words, to be a member of a children's group you have to know the linguistic, narrative structures to engage as a member of the group—you have to become recognisably the sort of person who should be included.

For example, if the group in question is in part defined through the adoption of hegemonic masculine practices, then it is extraordinarily difficult for a girl to gain access. Joanne liked to play with the dominant boys and her best friend, Tony, was one of them. But Joanne was rarely accepted into the boy's group as one of them, though she and I both gained complete access in an episode to be described later which I have called the 'Queen of the World' episode. Tony, for his part, wished to maintain his membership in the boys' group as well as his friendship with Joanne. This meant that Joanne had to have something extra to offer Tony that the boys did not have. Playing at her place in the afternoon turned out to be her major draw card. On one occasion Tony broke the rules associated with this, and Joanne was highly indignant. She said to me: 'I explained to Tony that if you say to somebody "I bet you don't want to come to my place this afternoon" and they say "yes", that you should play with them. You're not allowed to play with the others after you say yes' (observation notes, St Michael's).

When you don't have access to a friend of your choice, you can often rely on a contingency friend (Davies, 1982). I gained access to many conversations in this capacity. I could be used as a contingency friend since I was often sitting around on my own, I was a good listener, and I did not cling on to them when their real friend came along. They could talk to me while keeping an eye on the others' play, thus being ready to move back into play with others when the right moment occurred. Joanne sometimes used me in this capacity, and sometimes used Sandra. When Tony was playing with the boy's group she needed a contingency friend to cover the fact that she was waiting. Then when Tony joined her, she needed her contingency friend to go away because her company was no longer desirable, nor tolerable to Tony. Once Tony had joined Joanne and agreed to play with her, there was usually a very complex game played out to get rid of Sandra. Joanne and Tony would run off with Sandra chasing them. They would run inside one door and out another, usually managing to lose Sandra inside.

B.D.: (to Joanne and Tony) So you got rid of Sandra?
TONY: Yeah.
JOANNE: Yeah. I just had to be mean to Sandra. I went in that door and out that door and she thought—I bet she's still in there looking for me.
B.D.: Oh dear, poor Sandra.
JOANNE: We don't think poor do we?
B.D.: Don't you Tony?
JOANNE: No, 'cause I wanted her to stay in there somewhere. I do like her, I just

don't like her near me that much.

TONY: Yeah.

B.D.:   Is that because she doesn't play the way you do?

JOANNE: No, she just keeps following me, and I want her to go somewhere else, so I don't have to go with her.

TONY: Yeah. And we don't want, and ah, Joanne likes her sometimes, she likes going with her sometimes, but not all the time.

JOANNE: Yeah, I hate her following me, that's the way I hate her.

TONY: Not all the time.

JOANNE: No.

Because of the extent of unquestioned power that adults have over children, they can seriously impede children's agency or control of events, as the following example illustrates. In this episode Joanne is trying to move out of her play with Sandra and into play with Tony. This is being disrupted because Joanne's mother has decided that Tony can't come to their place because he might catch the illness that Joanne's sister has. Although Joanne is free to go to Tony's place, he does not accept this as a reasonable substitute. Joanne attempts to explain her mother's reasoning but this falls on deaf ears. At the same time poor Sandra is trying to gain some mileage out of her birthday which is coming up and is drawing on the authority of adults to ensure that the day will come off. The others are predictably scathing in response, not approving of this use of adult power in interactions in the playground:

(Joanne is playing on one of the climbing frames with Tony and David. Sandra is also climbing on the frame and is telling them about her birthday party to which everyone is invited. The others tell her that they are not coming.)

TONY: Oh, I don't think anyone will come.

(They talk to me briefly about how old they are and then Tony and David walk off talking to each other about their guns and Joanne follows them, saying in a cross voice to Sandra who trails after her: I'm not going, I don't want to go.)

SANDRA: Your mummy said yes so you've got to come to my party.

(Joanne walks away from her and comes to talk to me.)

B.D.:   Hello Joanne ... What was wrong with you on Tuesday?

JOANNE: I was sick. (She gives graphic details of her sickness.) Ellie (her sister) is still a bit sick. (She turns round and watches the boys on the climbing frame. She explains that Tony was supposed to come to her house today, but that her mother had said that he couldn't because he might catch the sickness from Ellie, but she had said that she could go to Tony's if she wanted to.)

B.D.:   So you have to go to his place?

JOANNE: If I want to.

B.D.:   And you don't want to?

JOANNE: No, I don't know yet.

B.D.:   You don't know yet? How will you make up your mind?

JOANNE: When preschool is finished, then I'll make up my mind.

B.D.:   Is Tony being nice to you today?

JOANNE: I bet he's going to be nice, because I only just came a while ago.

36

B.D.:   What's he doing now?

JOANNE: Going up there (on top of the fortress), and I don't want, he's just gone up there and I'll wait for him to come down.

B.D.:   Is he playing Voltron?

JOANNE: No.

B.D.:   What's he playing?

JOANNE: I don't know what he would be playing.

B.D.:   Why can't you go up there too?

JOANNE: 'Cause I don't, I'm too afraid to go up there.

B.D.:   Why?

JOANNE: I once tried to. I don't even try getting up there, 'cause they're always there. They can always see me coming up, so I stay down.

B.D.:   But aren't you their friend? Couldn't you go up there too?

JOANNE: Naa.

B.D.:   Why wouldn't they let you up?

JOANNE: I just don't want to go up.

(Joanne goes and plays with Sandra on the slippery dip. Meanwhile Tony is fighting with the other boys. I ask him what is happening, and it turns out his mind is not on his relationship with the boys, but on the fact that Joanne has said that he can't play at her place that afternoon. As soon as he starts to talk to me, Joanne joins us.)

TONY: We've got a whole box full of medicine!

JOANNE: Yeah, but that medicine mightn't help it. (then, to me) He hasn't got the right kind of medicine to help it, so he can't come.

B.D.:   (to Tony) Is Ellie still sick?

TONY: No.

(Joanne tries again to explain, but Tony goes off with Barry and Joanne with Sandra).

(audio transcript, St Michael's)

I include these stories here to show how tricky it is as adult to participate in this subtle, shifting, complex world of childhood relations. Adults can be a serious impediment to much of their play and so are not readily included. On one occasion, however, when I had been hanging around the edges of their play I got caught up in that play as a useful outsider. On this occasion I was granted child status and thus given the kind of access to their play that adults do not normally have. On this occasion (which I will elaborate in detail in Chapter 5 on male power) I was eventually quite shaken by the aggression that was let loose in my direction. When I became involved in their play I tried to develop strategies to defend and assert myself which did not involve positioning myself as powerful adult, but rather maintained my position as one of them, albeit with marginal outsider status. I also rejected the offers of help from a teacher who was brought to the scene by a concerned girl. After being attacked for some considerable time and trying a number of self-protective strategies, such as retreating to an area which I said was my safe hideaway (called 'bar' in my childhood), and finding that all known strategies failed, I resorted to climbing to the top of the climbing frame, announcing that I was Queen of the World and that there was nothing they could do to hurt me. This deeply outraged the boys who said, amongst other things:

DAVID: What if I punch you in the nose?
B.D.:   What if you punch me in the nose? No, I wouldn't even feel that.
TONY: But she'd have a bleeding nose, wouldn't she, Dave?
DAVID: Sure! Once I had a bleeding nose!
B.D.:   I couldn't feel David's punch I'm so powerful.
TONY: Yeah, let's do it both together, David!
B.D.:   I'm the Queen of the World.
TONY: Bang bang bang bang bang bang bang bang.
DAVID: You naughty girl, you're a little baby girl.
B.D.:   No, I'm the Queen of the World.
DAVID: Well we're not going to play, are we, Tony?
TONY: We're too powerful.
B.D.:   No, I'm more powerful than you.
BRIAN: You won't take anything.
TONY: We're not going to play with you.
BRIAN: You won't take anything.
B.D.:   I'm the most powerful person, nothing can touch me.
BRIAN: Well we're not going to play the game.
TONY: Aw.
B.D.:   Why? Why can't I be the most powerful?
BRIAN: Because! Then we, then then, you're so powerful.
DAVID: And then you win!
BRIAN: In the game.
DAVID: And then you win.
B.D.:   I should be able to win.
BRIAN: And we can't do anything to you.
TONY: And we don't want you to win.
B.D.:   I should be able to win.
BRIAN: No!

(audio transcript, St Michael's)

The narrative informing the game could not make any sense to the boys if I won. In refusing my correct positioning as victim in this game, I made a nonsense of it as far as the boys were concerned. Losing against other boys was presumably conceivable. Losing against a *solitary* female made no sense and their final defence was to refuse to play and thus to negate the element of the narrative that I was attempting to create in which a solitary female positioned as a child could have power.

Finding myself caught up in this way was an extraordinary experience of being in the child's world as a child. Like Bledsoe (1977–78), who describes becoming part of the world of the 'cave kids', I found that I could see quite differently once positioned as a child rather than an adult. Bledsoe says:

38

For the child the world is often a place for speculative fantasy. For the researcher, the child's world is often a suggestion, a remnant of another earlier order for himself or herself ... In most circumstances, when the adult world and the child's world intersect, the child's world is compromised. It is immediately converted into adult constructs. Abstract scientific categories are imposed upon a perceptual, primordial element of experience stored in the child's narrative structures. The prefigurative imagination that the researcher once had (and which is still available to the child) is no longer used for understanding. The suggestion and remnants of another earlier order are not part of the scheme of research. (1977–78:119)

Learning to see from the position of the child

The purpose of observing the children in the playground was to learn to see their meanings not filtered through a 'rational' adult lens, but rather to see them in terms of the children's lived experience with all its multiple positionings, its meanings, which cannot readily be encompassed in rational discourse because of the limitations in that discourse. What I learned to see and use again was the knowledge of multiple simultaneous discourses which include magic, logic and morality, and which draw on traditional narrative structures, adult symbolic systems and moral systems, as well as the children's own symbolic and moral orders.

In contrast to this experience of direct involvement, I often found myself asking, when watching the children, 'What on earth is going on here?' And I was heavily reliant on language, on symbolism, for apprehending the sense of their play. Sometimes the children would provide an explanation if they came to talk to me. But there was often no immediate answer, for neither they nor I could *say* what it was that was going on because we did not know how to find the words or concepts that would encapsulate the event. To this extent the children's world was as yet only partially shaped by language, by linguistic symbolic forms. And for this reason learning to interact with them on their own terms was of central importance.

This book is part of the symbolic world, it is a text, an object of the culture. It is, at the same time, a book written following an attempt to apprehend the unspoken, and to extend the symbolic structures to encompass more of the knowledge that I have as a result of attending to unspoken meanings.

Because I recorded the observations and the talk, I could come back to them repeatedly and bring to them the further experience, the unarticulated knowledge that I was developing, and on some occasions I could find words which made sense of what had seemed chaotic without appearing to distort or to lose the original event.

One such episode that involved crossing gender boundaries fascinated me at the time I observed it, but it was a long time before I felt I could really grasp or signify what was occurring. I wrote at the time:

> George was wearing a flimsy nylon skirt. I asked him how it made him feel and he answered 'powerful'. Another boy came over and punched him. He took the skirt off, rolled it up, tucked it under his arm and punched the boy back. I said, 'But George, if it makes you feel powerful why did you take it off to punch that boy?' He answered, 'No I didn't' and ran off. (observation notes, St Michael's)

How I eventually learned to construe this event was that I had unwittingly used, in this conversation with George, the patriarchal dualistic framework in which powerful had only one meaning, that is, male dominant physical strength. My question implied that male power was the only form of power. I had, I thought, 'caught him out' in an apparent error of logic. I now presume that he could not be powerful in a *male* sense while attired in female clothes, and had to retrieve his male symbol, trousers, to defend himself with physical aggression. As well, he may have been aware of the responsibility other children feel to ensure that others get their gender right, and that the punch, seemingly out of the blue, was to let him know he was in the wrong wearing a skirt. In order to deal with this early form of 'poofter-bashing', George needed to remove the source of the problem before dealing with it. To the extent that this was what he perceived himself as doing, my question was simply based on the wrong premise, and his answer makes perfect sense. What is significant here, however, is that while he had had the skirt on he had experienced a form of power that he equated with female symbolic forms. George also liked to wear superhero capes and butterfly capes and to run around with the cape floating behind him shouting, 'I am the power!' I don't know if long flowing skirts evoked the same experience of power as the capes or something different again, but there is a risk that my inability to understand what he was saying cast in doubt his experience of that different form of power. Through my own conceptual entrapment in the discursive practices available to me I potentially made it nothing, no power, male physical power being the only recognisable form. It is comforting to note, however, that George did reject my formulation, and that this is the case through all of the data where, as far as the children are concerned, I've got it wrong.

Although it is often my formulations of events that the children are asked to assent to or dissent from, the children understood that the form of discourse in which we were engaged was one in which it was appropriate to dissent if my formulations were wrong. Even so, my attempts at understanding George's behaviour and the activity of the boy who came and punched him are interpretable as category-maintenance work on my part—as a holding of the dualism in place. Some of the episodes in which category-maintenance work was taking place were extended over a long period of time and their meaning was not immediately visible at the time I observed them. The value of using a video-recorder to allow repeated viewings in which the fine detail could be picked up, recorded and analysed became particularly evident to me in relation to what I have called the 'Firefighter' episode. This episode extends over a period of more than one hour, and although I can now tell it as coherent story, it only became so after I had sifted out the overlapping action and interaction and the other parallel storylines that were being developed at the same time.

> Geoffrey and another boy dress up in the firefighters' coats and elaborate a game in which there is fire from which the girls can be saved or with which they can be destroyed. The girls enter into this and rush into the home corner saying, "quick, let's hide". At this particular point, the home corner was being videotaped. Nancy, who was doing the filming, after watching this particular sequence a couple of times, asked the girls why they couldn't be firefighters too and go and put out the fire. They toyed with this idea for some time, trying on firehats (back to front) and dressing their dollies in clothes that looked something like firefighters' clothes. Eventually, with dollies suitably attired, and in their strollers, they went off to fight the fire. Very soon they came running back into the home corner, tearful and shocked, saying, 'The boys burned our babies'. After a further period in the home corner they tried again and this time one of the boys physically attacked them, getting the toy gun and actually grinding it into one girl's neck, causing her considerable fear and pain. The girls attempted to turn the home corner into a stronghold, but the boys' aggression was too much for them and they eventually returned to their 'Quick, let's hide'. At this point the video camera catches a look of complete victory and delight written all over Geoffrey's face as he chases the girls into the home corner. (video notes, St Michael's)

The burning of the babies is a dramatic response to the attempt on the part of the girls to share with the boys the domination and control of the landscape that the boys take to be theirs. The girls' sphere of influence is in the domestic/internal/private spaces. There they can, to some extent, dictate their own terms. In the public sphere the boys are in control. They may allow the girls into the public spaces (in this case, certain sections of the playground), but there they dictate the terms or else force the girls back into the domestic sphere as they did in this episode. The fighting of fire as well as the use of guns is often seen by the boys as both heroic, saviour-type behaviour as well as aggressive and destructive. The girls are the ideal others to be saved and to be hurt—if they try to be 'male' players in the game there is no fun, no game. It was through incidents such as these and through the 'Queen of the World' episode that I could hear what Robbie was saying about how it was right to tease Oliver Button, and how although Oliver should do what he wanted to do, he, Robbie, would do no such thing.

The power of the narrative structures to create and sustain correct genderedness and the importance of being correctly gendered for social and emotional survival was something I experienced in the second stage of the study probably in much the same way I did as a child. The parallels between traditional story forms and playground play were extraordinary. Whether narrative forms can actually be changed becomes a pressing question. Cranny-Francis (1988) believes they cannot, but my research leaves me in no doubt that while the traditional narrative structures are extraordinarily difficult to think or feel beyond, we must nevertheless attempt to develop a new narrative form if children are to take us seriously when we tell them that bipolar oppressive male–female patterns are neither essential nor acceptable.

3 The sense children make of feminist stories

Childhood, it would appear, is a privileged time as far as the fantasy world is concerned, since children are quite deliberately presented with models of the world that are, at least on the surface of things, entirely fanciful. But the moral order is deeply embedded in that fanciful world. The division of the world into 'real' and 'fantasy' is itself an essential key to the establishment and maintenance of the moral order, since that which is 'incorrect' can be equated with the fantastical or unreal—with that which we could not or would not do (cf. Adams, 1986).

The order that children learn through narratives is one which provides both potential and constraint. As I have pointed out elsewhere (Davies, 1983b), children collude in the establishment of a particular social order since it provides a predictable social world through which they can know and be known. Favat sees children as turning to fairytales because they provide ordering devices which can then be applied to the chaos of their everyday worlds:

> Children's turning to the tale is no casual recreation or pleasant
> diversion; instead it is an insistent search for an ordered world more
> satisfying than the real one, a sober striving to deal with the crisis of
> experience they are undergoing. In such a view, it is even possible ... to
> see the child's turning to the tale as a salutary utilization of an implicit
> device of the culture. It would appear, moreover, that after reading a
> fairy tale, the reader invests the real world with the constructs of the tale.
> (Favat, 1977:62)

The division of the world into female and male is a consistent ordering device in children's stories. Through hearing traditional narrative children learn to recognise themselves and others as located within their own lived gendered narratives. Stories provide the metaphors, the characters and the plots through which their own

43

positionings in the social world can be interpreted.

Children's stories present them not only with the mundane gendered world of women in kitchens but also the fantasy world in which women escape kitchens and are beautiful and loved, their reward for which, is, of course, their own kitchen. If a woman is active and powerful she can only be accepted as such if her agency is directed in a *selfless* way towards a man or child whom she loves (see, for example, Aiken's *The Kingdom Under the Sea*). Men, in contrast, have a much more complex array of possibilities—their power is admired and celebrated, their strength and cleverness can be associated with negative or positive powers, even both at the same time, and their right of access to safe domestic spaces by no means depends on their virtue. The text of the story is generally a subtle and complex mixture of events that might really happen, and of events or characters that no-one is expected to hold open as a genuine possibility. The subtext is generally that which is assumed to be real. Gender relations, adult—child relations, relations between rich and poor, form the political message, the subtext, the ordered moral base on which stories, and thus the social world, are built.

The texts through which children are taught to read are usually based on a 'realistic' rather than a fantastical version of the world. Within this realistic world the man is presented as active agent in the outside world, and the woman as passive, supportive other. As well, a sickly sweet and middle-class version of the nuclear family is presented as the norm. Freebody and Baker (1987) show how children in beginning readers are usually male—female pairs and that the patterns of interaction between them constitute 'correct' maleness and femaleness. Some examples they give are as follows:

1. 'We have to jump this,' says Peter. 'Come after me. I know how to do it. Come after me, but keep out of the water.' Jane says, 'Mummy said that we must keep out of the water.' 'I know she said so,' says Peter, 'but we are not going in the water. I know how to do this.' Peter jumps again. 'You can do it, Jane,' he says. Then Jane jumps. She says, 'Yes, I can do it. Look at me, Peter, I can do it.'

2. 'I want to have a boat like this one day,' says Peter. 'You can have a big boat like this when you are a man,' says Jane. She puts a hat on Peter. It is Tom's hat. 'There you are,' she says. 'You look like a man now.'

3. 'Come and see this, Peter,' says Jane. 'Do come and look at this. It is the farm cat. Look what she has.' 'What fun,' says Peter. 'Will she let us play with her?' 'We will get her some milk,' says Jane.

How apparently innocently the male is constituted as the one who knows, the one who reasons and the one who leads, and the female as obedient, mindless, passive, rule-follower. The mother is the authority, left behind in the domestic space, and in this non-domestic space the boy's authority is greater. The girl is constituted

as achieving in the non-domestic space only through the encourage-
ment of the boy, and the boy is constituted as adult male through
the supportive work of the girl. The boy is the one who plays, who
has fun, and the girl empowers him through her nurturing behaviour
which facilitates his fun.

Much of the existing criticism of children's stories is fairly superficial and adopts what Walkerdine calls a limited 'rationalist' stance.
On a simple content analysis, the solution to Peter and Jane would
appear to present a problem only if Mummy is always left at home
and if Peter is always the leader. More subtle questions such as
Mummy's presumed responsibility for the moral order, Peter's right
(even obligation) to challenge that, the consistent male–female
coupling, are generally left unquestioned in such analyses. But as
Walkerdine says, a critique of children's stories should not be based
on attempts to insist that they should more accurately reflect the
real or the ideal world. We need, rather, to analyse the way in
which they provide a vehicle for children to discover ways of positioning themselves as a person: 'We need not point to some untainted reality outside the text, but to examine instead how those
practices within the text itself have relational effects that define who
and what we are' (Walkerdine, 1984:64). She goes on to say that
'the positions and relations created in the text both relate to existing
social and psychic struggle and provide a fantasy vehicle which
inserts the reader into the text' (1984:165).

Feminist analyses of stories, then, need to pay attention not only
to the content, but also to the metaphors, the forms of relationship,
the patterns of power and desire that are created in the text. How
the child relates to the text, inserts her or himself into the text, and
thus how she or he interprets and uses the text are also critical issues
for a feminist reading of children's texts.

Feminist stories for children are generally of two kinds. The first
is where the subtext is turned into the text—the story becomes a
story *about* gender. *Oliver Button Is a Sissy* falls into this category.
There is a risk with this kind of story, however, that the actual
storyline holds little interest for the children. A good example of
this failure occurs with the story *Arthur and Clementine*. In this
story Arthur and Clementine are two tortoises who fall in love and
get married. Clementine is an adventurous tortoise who wants to
travel and see the world. Arthur is more conventional and persuades
Clementine to stay at home while he goes to work. He showers her
with domestic gifts which are made part of the house on her back.
She is eventually so weighed down that she cannot move. All she
can do is dream of the things she might do. She is very unhappy but
Arthur thinks the solution is more gifts. He also starts to see her as
highly inadequate and tells her so. Eventually she sneaks out of her
'home' and goes adventuring and Arthur is left not knowing why his

wife has left him.

These stories fascinate those adults who have made gender relations a direct and analysable part of their everyday world. The
children do not tend to become involved in these essentially adult
stories at all since they are understandably not interested in the
problems of husbands and wives. Domesticity occurs, after all, after
the fantasy ends. It is the reward for female virtue and is therefore
difficult to problematise. An exception to this lack of interest was
shown by Anika whose parents were going through the process of
separation, so she lived in a family where domesticity had become
problematic and was therefore worthy of exploration through
narratives.

The second kind of feminist story is where gender relations remain
the subtext, but where the metaphors through which the children
have come to understand being female or male are shifted, such that
a new kind of narrative is made possible. Zipes says of such stories
that their purpose is to disrupt the conserving values and rules of the
civilising process, that is, to disrupt the moral order. He distinguishes
between transfiguring the classical fairytale so that the storyline
remains the same but a different set of values is introduced (for
example, a rewriting of *Little Red Riding Hood* such as that by Lee,
1983), and transfiguring through a fusion of traditional configura-
tions with contemporary references. *The Paper Bag Princess* falls
into this second category. Of this kind of story Zipes says:

> Fantastic projections are used here to demonstrate the changeability of
> contemporary social relations, and the fusion brings together all the
> possible means for illuminating a concrete utopia. In effect, the narrative
> techniques of fusion and transfiguration are aimed at disturbing and
> jarring readers so that they lose their complacent attitude toward the
> status quo ... (Zipes, 1982:316)

We have good historical analyses to show that there is nothing
sacred or absolute about the current form of traditional fairytales.
The modern 'sanitised' Walt Disney versions of the fairytales are a
relatively recent phenomenon, which can and arguably should be
changed in keeping with modern developments in gender relations
(Zipes, 1986). Some of these reworkings are included in Zipes
(1986) and make fascinating reading. In fact, dozens of feminist
stories for children have been produced in the last decade or so (see
Appendix).

But neither feminist versions of old stories nor new feminist
stories are readily available in bookshops and libraries, and schools
show almost no sign of this development. Many parents and teachers
are thus unaware of the alternatives that are available. Yet feminist
stories are an invaluable resource for the imaginative construction of
subject positionings outside of traditional gendered relations. The

bulk, if not all, of the stories that children hear have as their sub—text sexist and class-based constructions of reality. These stories are a critical resource through which children learn to constitute themselves as bipolar males or females with the appropriate patterns of power and desire.

The particular stories used in this study were selected on the following bases:

1 They were readily available, if only from feminist bookstores.
2 They were attractively presented and illustrated so as to engage children's interest.
3 They were to deal with a variety of feminist issues, including problems relating to masculinity.
4 They were to be written with four- and five-year-old children in mind.
5 They were well written and not overtly moralistic and pedantic.
6 The children of my study at the same time wanted to hear and enjoyed hearing them.
7 They were useful in generating discussions in which the children's understanding of gender could be elaborated.

Using the first three criteria, I selected 50 or so stories. This was then narrowed down to a dozen when the fourth and fifth points were taken into account, and was eventually narrowed down to four stories when the sixth and seventh criteria were explored. Some excellent stories, such as *Princess Smartypants*, I did not find until after I had collected my data and so are not included in the study. The children's responses to the four stories, *Oliver Button Is a Sissy, The Princess and the Dragon, Rita the Rescuer* and *The Paper Bag Princess*, form the basis of this chapter.

Children use their own experiences in the everyday world and their knowledge of other stories in relation both to characters and plot to make sense of the stories they hear (Applebee, 1978). This relates both to text and subtext—to what happens in stories and to what is understood about the forms or relations and ways of being through which the text is created. Although each story presents new possibilities it is interpreted in terms of what is already known, not just known consciously about the way the world is organised, but also known through the metaphors and the patterns of power and desire that are implicated in the narrative structures.

Feminist stories are about providing narrative structures in which new ways of resolving existing conflicts are presented. Because of the complexity of this task it is inevitable that some of them fall short of the mark. The feminist story is constrained by something of a double bind: if the primary focus is just on new images and the story fails to confront the issues and conflicts surrounding gender as it is experienced and understood, then it cannot adequately generate new possibilities. But to work from what is already known and apprehended inevitably means that the story is constructed out of, and thus potentially confirms, the very metaphors and attendant forms of relations that need to be worked beyond.

Oliver Button Is a Sissy

Oliver Button Is a Sissy appears at first to be a good feminist story, and certainly the children liked it. The intention of the story is to show that boys can be 'feminine', that they do not have to be traditionally masculine to be acceptable. Such a story is necessarily grounded in the male—female duality, since it is one half of the duality that Oliver is struggling to extend so that it includes elements of the other. The feminist message of the story is that although it may be a struggle for a male to adopt 'feminine' ways of being because of all the category-maintenance work that will go on around him, it is nonetheless possible not only to do so and be accepted but even to be celebrated. But many children interpret the male—female dualism as being confirmed through this story since the major part of it is about the trauma of being subjected to category-maintenance work by one's father and by the boys at school. In part this is a linguistic problem as the story invites talk about 'girls' things' and 'boys' things' as if they were clearly separate and identifiable. The story is thus one which may further reify for the children their understanding of the current gender order. On the other hand, though the language itself confirms existing assumptions of difference, it is possible that the discussion around the story breaks the categories open to a certain extent.

The story begins with a detailed statement to the effect that Oliver Button likes to do girl's things instead of the things that boys are supposed to do. This distresses his father who begs him to do boys' things instead: '"Oliver," said his Dad. "Don't be such a sissy! Go out and play baseball or football or basketball. Any kind of ball!"' But Oliver declines on the grounds that he is hopeless at ball games and that he can easily keep fit doing the things he likes to do such as dancing. Eventually his parents agree to let him go to dancing classes, '"Especially for the exercise," says his Dad.' Oliver loves dancing, but the boys at school give him a really hard time and write on the school wall 'OLIVER BUTTON IS A SISSY'. Oliver keeps on dancing and his teacher suggests that he go in a talent quest. He dances well but he does not win the talent quest. His parents and teachers still think he is great, but Oliver is very downcast and does not want to go to school the next day. When he gets to school, however, the boys have crossed out 'SISSY' and written 'STAR'. The new message on the wall is 'OLIVER BUTTON IS A STAR'.

The ending is very puzzling for the majority of children who hear it. They have no idea why the boys changed their mind and the authors do not provide any possible way into this understanding. The most obvious interpretation, and one that Anika came up with, is that the teachers told them to do it. Another, produced by Robbie, comes from the traditional male logic that it's all right to do female things as long as you are better than everyone else at them. The problem with this interpretation is that Oliver is not the best since he not only doesn't win but, to make matters worse, he nearly cries about it. The fact that his parents and teacher love him is entirely in keeping with the expected pattern that boys will be seen by adults to have potential no matter what they do (Adams and Walkerdine, 1986). But Oliver is hopeless at boy's things. He is readily interpretable as a failed male, who is allowed to do girls' things in order to maintain one essential aspect of his masculinity— his fitness. Oliver is not someone the boys want to position themselves as, as the discussion with Robbie illustrated in Chapter 2.

The majority of children who listened to this story asserted, like Robbie, that boys should do boys' things and girls should do girls' things. Even Joanne, who obviously preferred boys' things, made this assertion while listening to this story and produced 'proofs' of her own femininity by telling me that she liked to play at being mother to her little sister and that she liked to play with her Barbie doll. Most of the children asserted that Oliver Button should not do girls' things, no matter how much he hates boys' things and no matter how much he wants to do girls' things. Despite the fact that many of them really empathised with Oliver, they could not positively place themselves in his position or claim that they would support him. Kennard (1986) points out that it is possible to engage in what she calls a polar reading of the text—that is, the listener moves into the position of the central character during the reading of the story but then uses that experience to say that this is what I am not. Through a polar reading one clarifies who one is in opposition to, rather than in consonance with, the hero.

In talking about Oliver Button there was some slight overlap between what the children thought girls' and boys' things might be since some thought it all right for boys to pick flowers and some thought it all right for girls to play football, and one noted that both could do gymnastics, but in general they claimed that the legitimate fields of activity were separate and distinct. Boys were not to pick flowers, dress dolls, play with paper dolls, sing or dance (that is, all the things that Oliver Button liked to do). They should do karate, play with guns, play cricket and play with Lego, put jeans on, play soccer and football and play in the dirt. As Jenny (from Lothlorien) said, in response to my questions:

'(If you were Oliver, and you were a boy and you really loved to dance, would you go to dancing school?) No. (But if you hated playing ball would you still play it even though you hated it?) No I wouldn't. (What

49

would you do?) Go to gymnastics. (Can boys and girls go to gymnastics?) Yeh.' And Elise (from Lothlorien): 'I know a girl who likes to do boy things and they call her dilly dummy. (Who's that?) Just a girl who likes to play with Lego.'

Because of the way children are positioned, that is, as incomplete persons who do not yet fully know or understand the moral/social order, much of their experience is of being told they have erred. To be accorded full human status they must avoid being caught out in such errors. Much of the fear and anxiety of childhood is connected with the process of acquiring 'correct' behaviours, 'correct' language, 'correct' personhood. Characters in their everyday world as well as the characters in books are an important resource in learning to get it right:

1　My dad's a boy. (Would your dad say go out and do things boys do and play ball?) Yes and I would do that. (You would? If you were wanting to dress up and play with paper dolls and your dad said, 'Sebastian, go outside and do what boys do and play with the cricket bat and football'?) I would do that. (Sebastian)

2　(Why didn't Oliver Button like to play ball?) 'Cause he doesn't play it right. (Are you supposed to want to do the things that other boys or other girls do, are you?) You do what you're told.　(Katy)

3　(What if they hated baseball and karate and they wanted to go to ballet? What would happen then?) The mother might keep him home and smack his bottom. (Why should she do that?) Because he's a bad boy. (Hamid, Inner City)

Other children who are erring in ways that one has learned not to err need to have their errors pointed out to them. The term 'peer pressure' does not capture what it is the children are doing here, since it lends the wrong emphasis, suggesting the children have decided independently of the social/moral order that other children should conform to it. What the children say about the way Oliver Button is treated can best be understood as the children engaging in the maintenance of the moral order through which the patterns of power and desire, that they have taken up as part of their ways of being, are maintained as meaningful.

The moral order is not experienced as an external imposition, it is experienced as a set of self-evident meanings through which the world and one's various positionings within it are maintained. Thus the division of the world into male and female does not need to be explained, it just is: '(Why did his dad say that?) Cause he's not a girl, he's a boy'. (Elise, Lothlorien)

At the same time, as I showed with Robbie in Chapter 2, that self-evident structure can nevertheless be experienced as running counter to some aspects of personal desire, and so its status as a given is never fully secured. Although gender is taken up as personal, as one's own, it is also experienced as a public possession, and although it is taken to be self-evident, a great deal of category-maintenance work needs to be done on it to keep it intact.

1 '(Why did they say sissy to him?) Because they think he's a boy. (And so if he's a boy isn't he allowed to dance?) No.' (Robbie)

2 '(Do you think boys are allowed to do the things that girls do?) No. (Why not?) They are not allowed to. (Who wouldn't let them?) Those guys tease him.' (Jane, Moore St)

The idea of behaving publicly like the 'opposite' gender was for most laughable and silly:

'(Why did his dad say that?) Because he's not a girl. (But why can't a boy do what Oliver wants to do if he likes doing it?) It's not OK. (Why isn't it OK?) Because he's not a girl, and he puts girls' clothes on. He looks silly and his name will be poo poo or silly.' (Louise, Inner City)

This feeling of silliness becomes so much part of your psychic structure that you might even find yourself laughing at yourself if you behave like the 'wrong' sex, as Anika so graphically explains:

'when people, when the wrong kind of human being does that, I get a tickle in my brain ... (And what about if a girl does a boy thing?) I get the same thing ... and it makes me laugh ... it's like a little man is in my brain tickling my brain ... it's like a piece of string like this tickling from side to side.'

The power of names is also quite interesting, and naming seems to have a circular and inevitable logic which suggests that the risks attached to being named something are quite high:

1 (Why did they say sissy?) Because they thought he was one.' (Jill, St Michael's)

2 (Why did he like to do all those things?) Because he was called a sissy. (Why did the boys say sissy?) Because his name's sissy. (No, his name is Oliver Button. Why do you think they said sissy?) Because he did all this dancing.' (John, Inner City)

Some girls envisaged that they would join in the teasing or displayed the kind of teasing they would do while they were talking about it:

I (If those big boys were your friends, Kim, and they wanted to tease Oliver, would you tease him too and call him a sissy?) (nods) (And if you saw him looking like that [sad] how would you feel?) I'd still tease him.

2 They [boys] don't pick flowers. (David says he picks flowers.) Then [to David] you're a sissy. (Why shouldn't he pick flowers?) He's a boy. (You don't think that boys should pick flowers?) No. (Why not?) Because they're stupid boys. (But they're nice boys.) No, they're fucky boys. (Elise, Lothlorien)

Thus people who behaved outside of their assigned gender were to be censured, and punished, no matter how painful that might be for them as individuals, and no matter how much, privately, they might enjoy 'incorrect' activities. For some, this imperative appeared to be accompanied by a recognition that gender is, after all, only an achievement, and that failure to behave in the 'correct' way might mean you can no longer make claims to be the gender you were originally assigned:

1   (Why did his dad say that?) Because he's a boy. (And are boys supposed to go outside and play football?) Yep. (Why does his dad think that?) Because he thinks he's going to become a girl. (Do you think he would be if he did all those things?) Mmm. (George, St Michael's)

2   (Why did his dad say that?) Because he wants to marry someone . . . some girls and boys they're allowed to marry girls . . . but he should marry a girl, a nice girl. (Hamid, Moore St)

3   (Why did his dad say that?) Because he's pretending he's a girl . . . he's doing girls' things. (Do you think his dad thinks it's a problem?) Yes, 'cause he, I think his dad, um, thinks he wants to be a tomboy. (Do you think his dad might be unhappy if he wants to be a tomboy?) Mmmm.' Cause he just wants a boy called Oliver Button. (Anika)

These children recognise (like Agnes, in Garfinkel's [1967] significant work on the achievement of sex status in an 'intersexed' person) that genderedness is an ongoing achievement, though, as Agnes realised, it is not so much a private achievement as a public one. It is to do with relations with others, not with who you think you might privately like to be. What you are taken to be is what you are. You cannot just be sort of one or the other, and you cannot be one but behave like the other. Maleness and femaleness are exclusive *relational* categories and competent social membership requires that you be, that is, behave in relation to others as if you are, one or the other.

There were, however, two boys, Mark and Daniel (Inner City), both of whose parents refused sexist discourse as legitimate discourse, who did not support this consistent dualistic line. They both engaged in 'feminine' behaviours and claimed that they saw nothing wrong with this. They believed not only that Oliver Button should have been free to go to dancing school but that the older boys should have left him alone. Mark and Daniel both went to dancing lessons themselves, not like Oliver because they desperately wanted to, but because their parents were very keen that they not be caught up in 'masculine' activities to the exclusion of 'feminine' activities. In the conversation that follows, Mark is accompanied by Leo's three-year-old sister, Kim:

B.D.:   Is he nearly going to cry?
MARK: Yes.
B.D.:   He doesn't like being called a sissy, does he?

MARK: (shakes head)

B.D.:   Would you call someone a sissy if they went to dancing lessons? (interruption)

B.D.:   Right. If those big boys were your friends, Kim, and they wanted to tease Oliver, would you tease him too and call him a sissy?

KIM: (nods)

B.D.:   You would? Um, and if you saw him looking sad like that, how would you feel?

KIM: I'd still tease him.

B.D.:   You'd still tease him, and why would you do that? (silence) If those big boys were your friends ... and what about you, Mark, if those big boys were your friends and they were teasing Oliver, would you tease him too?

MARK: No.

B.D.:   What would you do?

MARK: I would, I would stop them.

B.D.:   Would you? What would you say to them?

MARK: I dunno.

B.D.:   You don't know? You'd just manage to stop them somehow?

MARK: Mmm.

B.D.:   (reads about how Oliver Button went to dancing school and practised and practised) Is that the right thing for him to do, to keep on going to the dancing school?

MARK and KIM: Yes.

B.D.:   Why was it the right thing to do?

MARK: Because he couldn't [learn to] dance himself.

B.D.:   He couldn't what?

MARK: Because he couldn't dance himself.

B.D.:   Because he couldn't dance he had to go to Miss Leah to learn how?

MARK: Yes.

B.D.:   And if you had been Oliver Button would you have kept going to dancing school, Mark?

MARK: Yes.

B.D.:   Even though the boys teased you?

MARK: Mmm.

B.D.:   What about Kim, would you keep going to the school even though the boys teased you?

KIM: (shakes head)

Mark claims that he would stop the older boys from teasing Oliver, though when asked how he would do this he said he didn't know. When we had finished recording I asked him again and said that he would just talk to them and tell them not to do it. Later he said that that is what adults would tell you to do, but it would be more effective to throw sticks at them; that is, ironically, one would have to resort to "masculine" behaviours to undo category-maintenance work around masculinity. Mark and Daniel had made the critical step of giving up the idea of male and female as dualistic and could take up feminine positionings without finding this incompatible with who they took themselves to be. Although they were also interested in masculine positionings and although they were in no doubt at all about the centrality of maleness to their identity, a central feature of maleness—its opposition to femaleness —was not a feature for them.

To what extent this story could convince anyone to move in this direction I am not all sure. The story itself does not have a sufficiently convincing ending to counteract the bouts of category-maintenance work that Oliver suffers. The story's main value, as far as I can see, is in its capacity to open up discussion about Oliver's experience and thus to make the way gender relations are created something that can be analysed and thus potentially changed.

The Princess and the Dragon

The second story, *The Princess and the Dragon*, is about a princess who doesn't like being a princess, who is messy, rude and who makes life difficult for everyone around her, and a dragon who doesn't like being a dragon because it dreams of doing ballet and 'playing the violin with its eyes closed'. When the dragon comes to town everyone is frightened. The princess decides to go to the dragon's cave in order to be caught, so that the poor old knight, who is afraid of the dragon, will have to go to the trouble of saving her. The princess is amazed to discover the dragon playing the piano. This dragon is not like a dragon at all. The princess and the dragon swap places, each becoming what they really want to be. Everyone is delighted with the new, sugar-sweet, super-polite 'princess', who says things like, 'Good morning, isn't it a lovely day?', 'Please pass the butter' and, to the cook, 'Simply divine. May I have seconds please?' As well, they are able to put up with the new 'dragon' who gets up to mischief but does not really worry anyone (except the knight whom she captures). 'The King and Queen are overjoyed at the change' and 'all the mothers and fathers in the kingdom told their children to behave like the Princess.' The 'princess' and the 'dragon' become great friends and at the end of the story the two friends, along with all the children in the village, are having a party at the cave, this being the new place to go when they cannot behave themselves like the new princess.

The feminist message is that people should be able to be what they want to be, and will be happy if the world is organised to allow them to be so. But again it is not necessarily heard that way by the children. Almost all the children who listened to this story liked and preferred the sugar-sweet dragon who behaved as children are supposed to behave, that is, like the three boys in their yellow raincoats and rain hats in Chapter 1, politely shaking the teacher's hand and saying 'Good afternoon'. Almost none liked the rough, tough princess who broke the adult rules for child behaviour and became a dragon. The story is seen by most of the children as being about a goodie and a baddie, and they have no sympathy whatsoever for the princess cast in the baddie role. She is described by the children as 'dirty, mean, naughty, a pig, yukky, ugly, horrible, a bum, terrible, poking her tongue out and with awful hair'. Princesses are supposed to be, they say, good, beautiful and nice, and they are supposed to smile, to have beautiful hair and to get married. Several girls, including Joanne, said 'she is supposed to be like me'.

That one would want to be good seemed unquestionable to all of them, except Natasha from Inner City: '(If you were a princess and you hated it, what would you do?) I'd be a dragon. If I was a real dragon I could kill people who I don't like.'

Occasionally some of the more dominant boys would say in jest that they would like to be like the bad princess, but they made it clear they were joking, even though the 'bad' princess achieves a form of behaviour quite close to the hegemonic masculinity that they display. But only once did a boy falter over choosing the more 'feminine' princess. My assertion that he could take up a feminine fantasy was clearly outrageous to him:

> I want to be the princess. (Yes.) I'm not really a girl am I? (No, but boys can pretend to be princesses.) No! (Sometimes they can, they can put a dress on and play at being princess. 'Cause girls can dress up and pretend to be boys can't they?) No! (Why can't you be a princess?) I don't want to. (Would you if you wanted to?) No, I want to be Superman. (Llewellyn, Lothlorien)

Most children did not even agree that it would be fun to go up into the dragon's cave, which is defined, at the end of the story, as the place children like to go when they feel like being naughty:

> '(Do all those children like being up there when they want to be naughty and bad?) Ah, they don't want to be bad, they want to be like the dragon princess. (Do you ever be noisy and bad like those children here?) No.' (Sebastian)

This response seemed to me, at first, rather puzzling as the dragon is really nauseatingly sweet and polite, and the princess is full of life and fun and rather like an exaggerated version of the vast majority of children in the study, although more powerful. The children, both male and female, were intensely aware, however, of the adult requirement that they be good, and the story is for them located in the moral subtext of adult−child relations rather than male−female relations. Within this moral order one may be naughty, but one cannot conceivably *want* to be naughty. What one wants within the adult−child moral framework is to be liked or loved by the adults involved:

> '(Do you feel happiest when you are being naughty like her, or good like the dragon?) I like to be good like the dragon. (Do you? Is that because Mummy likes you best when you're good like the dragon, or because you like you best?) Mummy likes me.' (Katy)

Most parents would be amazed to discover the depth of this desire to be good. As Walkerdine and Lucey (1989) show, the persuasion/manipulation/coercion that mothers engage in to bring about correct behaviour in their children involves a continual battle of wills. Gabrielle talks quite casually about one such scenario in her own household:

> Sometimes I shout so loud I have to block my own ears. (Do you think Mummy would like a place like the dragon's cave where you could go when you want to be noisy?) Uh huh. (Where do you go at home when you want to be noisy?) In the backyard and Mummy locks the door so we can't come in. (Uh huh. Does she say, 'go outside and shout'?) Oh, she says, right, if we won't go outside she is going to run away.

Essentially *The Princess and the Dragon* is heard by the children as a story about a good dragon who was able to be what the adults wanted it to be ('The King and Queen were overjoyed by the change') and it was suitably rewarded for its goodness by being allowed to live in the castle and be loved and cossetted and admired by everyone. The bad princess, in contrast, is banished to the cave (in the same way that Gabrielle is sent outside) to live on her own. The narrative structure in which good girls are rewarded by a secure and happy family-type situation makes it difficult for the children to hear the alternative narrative form in which it is good for people to be what they want to be. Even the boys are sufficiently caught up in the fantasy of being so much what their parents want in order to be loved and cherished unstintingly that they readily place themselves in the position of the dragon who became the princess, regardless of gender and regardless of its 'prissy' version of femininity. As well, the dualistic construction of goodies and baddies implicit in traditional narrative structures makes it difficult to see that the princess is not a baddie when put in the right situation, particularly since she continues to get up to mischief. The adult−child subtext is clearly a powerful one in its ability to override the gender subtext and the liberal humanist subtext of individualism and freedom.

Rita the Rescuer

The third story, *Rita the Rescuer*, is the story of a girl who is always being left out of things by her big brothers and sisters. One day when she is left all alone at home someone mysteriously leaves a superhero outfit on the front-door-step. She is able, in the guise of Rita the Rescuer, to rescue her older brothers and sisters as well as others in the community when they get themselves into trouble, or find themselves in some kind of distress. Rita keeps the outfit a secret so that her brothers and sisters do not know that she is the famous rescuer. *Rita the Rescuer* can be seen at first glance to fit into the category of story that Walkerdine (1984) warns against where only the image is changed, that is, where the girl is simply portrayed doing the things that boys normally do. Walkerdine warns that this device can alienate girls as much as switch them on to the new possibilities. However, when examined carefully, what Rita does when she gets her rescuer's outfit is 'feminine' and therefore not alienating, since she uses her superpowers not to dominate and control, nor to bring glory to herself, but simply to help others, even those who have hurt her. Rita the Rescuer fits closely with Zipes' description of the hero in feminist tales:

> the structure of most of the feminist tales is based on the self definition of a young woman. The female protagonist becomes aware of a task which she must complete in social interaction with others to define herself. Instead of pursuing power for the purpose of self aggrandisement or omnipotence, the heroine rejects violence and seeks to establish her needs in harmony with the needs of others. Power will only be used in self defence or to prevent violence. Though the heroine may be wronged, she will rarely seek revenge ... the aesthetic form is derived from nurturing rather than competition. (Zipes, 1986:32)

The children like this story very much and most of them readily identify with Rita, though the boys, more used to positioning themselves as superheroes, are able to engage in the story in more detail than are the girls. The boys tend to ignore the fact that Rita is a girl—her gender, for them, not being a feature of the story. Their responses to this story put one in mind of Connell's statement that 'the physical sense of maleness grows through a personal history of social practice, a life-history-in-society' (1987:84). They readily understand the detail of Rita's various rescues and comment on them on the way through. Some volunteer that they are going to be superman when they grow up, and Mark says he has superpowers already since he is very good at schoolwork. With one exception, they readily say they would like to be Rita and to have her outfit. They talk about how good it would be to fly, they tell about their flying dreams, they flex their muscles to show how strong they are and fall to wrestling each other on the floor to display their strength. In other words, they insert themselves into the story as if they were Rita, they do not relate to Rita as other, nor to Rita as a hard-done-by girl, but as Rita the Rescuer who is like them. George loved the story so much that he carried the book around with him whenever I didn't need it.

The girls, in contrast, are much more aware of the fact that Rita is a girl. They are careful to use the terms 'supergirl' and 'superwoman' in describing her, in contrast with the boys who were just as likely to use the term 'superman'. The girls, with some exceptions, thought they would like to be like Rita and have a rescuer's outfit, but had very little physical or imaginary conception of themselves as appropriately strong. They could not flex their muscles to show them off, even when I showed them how, and they could not imagine flying. Even the girls who were observably strong, active and agile and who easily held their own with the boys lacked a concept of themselves as strong, and certainly had no concept of *displaying* themselves as strong. There were some exceptions, most notably from two of the Moore St girls. Lily said she liked the story because it made her 'lips go dry' and that Rita was 'a nice rescue girl'. She would 'like to have a outfit like she made' and she would 'fly up and rescue things, whoever's in trouble'. And Karen declared she didn't even need a rescuer's outfit to be as brave as Rita: she would deal with the bullies 'by just kicking them in the tummy and running away fast and climbing up a tree which they would fall down'. At the other extreme were the girls at Inner City, Sharon, Natasha and Marilla, who showed almost no interest in Rita, but were captivated by 'the lady who's getting married' who was one of the people Rita saved. They fought over which one of them could be the bride, and then agreed that one could be the baby that was saved and one the 'little white kitten'. Rita was not someone they even contemplated positioning themselves as.

For the rest, they enjoyed the idea of being a hero, but did not seem to have the bodily knowledge and awareness that could make the fantasy anything other than a passing interest. Sebastian makes an observation relevant to this point. He says: 'How come Rita is getting longer legs now she's getting lots of exercise? (She probably is too.) Then she'll be able to play games like Rita, just pretending to be superman.'

It is not, at this point in their lives, that the girls are generally physically weaker than the boys. It is that they have not developed fantasies around the idea of being strong and thus do not know how to project their bodies into the world in powerful ways, either in fact or in imaginary games (see Young, 1980). They are competent, strong and agile, with some exceptions as there are amongst the boys, but their lack of relevant fantasies may prevent them extending that competence and using it in powerful and assertive ways. It may also prevent them from defending themselves against aggressors because they cannot imagine themselves physically able to do it. Haug comments: 'It is precisely because we gain in competence through our bodily practices that we cling to them as we do. The drawback, however, is that in exercising this power, we simultaneously confine ourselves to one part of a wider world and one particular relationship to it' (1987:27).

Thus the story of Rita does provide an imaginary possibility, though one, ironically, more easily taken up by the boys than the girls. This taking up, on the part of the boys, of a female heroic position is, however, of central importance in developing narrative structures which dissociate maleness from masculine positionings, both in the sense that they position themselves as female hero and in the sense that Rita is both female and heroic. For the girls who position themselves as Rita, however, the story is more complicated. It provides a narrative structure organised around a girl with strength and physical power, who can legitimately be positioned as hero, though only in private. This self-effacement chosen by Rita may well undermine the value of the story for girls, in that it confirms the idea that women can only be powerful or agentic in private.

Interestingly, the categories female and male are not called on strongly to support the fabric of the story. Indeed, they are almost irrelevant, at least as far as Rita is concerned—she is presented in overalls and holding a doll at the beginning—although the other characters are presented in traditional male and female activities, with some notable exceptions, such as boys and girls skipping together. When Rita is left alone at the beginning by her adventuring older brothers and sisters, then, it is not because she is a girl, but because she is too young, though the characteristics ascribed to her age category are also the characteristics usually ascribed to girls: '"Take me with you," begged Rita one day. "You're too young," said Eddie, "you can't push or pull." "You're too young," said Jim. "You can't run or kick." "You're too young," said Julie. "You can't skip or jump."' Thus with a subtext of age relations, gender categories and relations are subtly shifted to enable Rita to deal with her inferior position in the age relations with her brothers and sisters.

The Paper Bag Princess

The Paper Bag Princess, the fourth of the stories to be dealt with here, also at first sight appears to be a simple reversal in which the female is given a typical male hero's role in which the hero displays public bravery and publicly fights against injustice, but it is a story with many subtle twists and an unexpected ending. This is by far the children's favourite story, though few of them understand its feminist message, at least on the first few readings.

In this story Princess Elizabeth is the hero who takes on the dragon in order to save Ronald. The intention here is to present a female hero who is not dependent on the prince in shining armour for her happiness nor for confirmation of who she is. It also casts serious doubt on the concept of the prince who can provide eternal happiness. In this story Elizabeth is not a unitary being. She experiences the multiple and contradictory subject positionings we each experience in our everyday lives. She is positioned at the beginning as the uncomplicated, happy and loving princess, living out the romantic narrative of love and happiness ever after. She is then positioned as the dragon's victim, but rejects this positioning and becomes the active, heroic agent who is in control of the flow of events. She is then positioned as victim again by Ronald and again refuses this positioning, skipping off into the sunset, a free agent.

When the dragon burns Elizabeth's castle and steals Prince Ronald, he also burns her clothes off and makes her very dirty. Most children see her at this point as having magically changed into a bad princess, as if the dragon had cast a spell on her. That badness, because of her nakedness, has negative sexual overtones. Some of the boys are very switched on to her naked and bereft state and are fascinated by the large, powerful and destructive dragon who has devastated her and later goes on to devastate entire landscapes. Other boys constitute Ronald as hero. Most are unable to see Elizabeth as a genuine hero, and are equally unable to see her choice to go it alone at the end as legitimate or positive. The dragon, for most, is the powerful lascivious male, whose power remains untainted by Elizabeth's trickery. In this version of the narrative Elizabeth clearly loses her prince, not because she chooses to leave him, but because she is lacking in virtue. Most children believed Elizabeth should have cleaned herself up and then married the prince.

An early piece of analysis that I undertook in the first stage of the data-collection (Davies, 1987) suggested that those children who had a mother who worked in the paid workforce also had access to interpretive possibilities that were of critical importance in being able to comprehend the feminist meanings of stories such as *The Paper Bag Princess*. Taking each child's comments about the characters, their motives and the storyline in *The Paper Bag Princess*, it is possible to see that the story that is heard is subtly different for each child, this difference relating in part to the subject position she/he takes up in the story (positioning her/himself as Elizabeth or Ronald or the dragon) and in part on her/his understanding of gender relations.

The girls' understandings

Anika's story
Princess Elizabeth loves Prince Ronald, but 'he's just ignoring her, and she's putting all her love to him and that's wasting her love'.

The dragon burns the castle down and carries off Prince Ronald. Princess Elizabeth 'feels angry'.

Elizabeth plans to make the dragon 'really tired by making him do all the things lots of times'.

Ronald is 'a mean person', so Elizabeth is 'rude' to him.

They are both angry and so they are not going to marry each other. This is the correct decision, at least for the time being.

Anika says she would like to be like Princess Elizabeth.

Gabrielle's story

Princess Elizabeth is a 'nice' and 'beautiful' princess who is going to marry Prince Ronald.

The dragon burns her castle and clothes and crown and carries off Prince Ronald.

Elizabeth plans to 'follow the dragon on these trails'. 'She wants to talk to the dragon' and 'she is going to trick him'.

Princess Elizabeth is pleased that she is not going to marry Ronald because he is not a nice person. This is the correct decision.

Gabrielle says she would like to be like Elizabeth, though preferred her at the beginning rather than the end.

Katy's story

Princess Elizabeth and Prince Ronald are married. She has beautiful clothes.

The dragon burns the castle down and Ronald disappears. Elizabeth 'follows the dragon ...' cause he's got Ronald'.

She makes the dragon tired. She is a 'dirty' princess.

Prince Ronald quite rightly tells Elizabeth to go away and get changed 'and come back when she's more like a real princess'. If she had done so, the original happy order would have been re-established, even though Ronald is not a nice person.

She would like to be like Princess Elizabeth.

Summary of girls' understandings

Anika, Gabrielle and Katy all place themselves in the position of the princess. They see her as nice, beautiful, etc. All three understand her plan. All three see Ronald as not very nice, although Katy differs significantly from the other two in believing that Elizabeth should have done as Ronald told her.

The boys' understandings

Sebastian's story

A prince and princess are about to get married.

The dragon burns the castle and Ronald is high up in the air. Ronald very cleverly holds on to his tennis racquet tightly which is why he stays up in the air. Elizabeth and Ronald are both angry. The dragon goes home.

Elizabeth 'tricks' the dragon 'because she wants to get her prince back'.

Prince Ronald tells Elizabeth to clean herself up 'because

61

he didn't like her being so messy'. He is a nice person and she should clean herself, just as Sebastion has to do when he is dirty, no matter how hard it is to get the dirt off. It is all right that they don't marry each other because 'he married some-one else'.

Sebastian says he would like to be Prince Ronald.

Robbie's story
Prince Ronald is a tennis player. 'He's got a tennis jumper and he won the tennis gold medal.' He is 'shy' and he doesn't want to marry Princess Elizabeth.

The dragon burns off Elizabeth's clothes, breaks her tower and burns the trees and flies off with Prince Ronald.

Elizabeth is 'cross'.

Elizabeth 'follows the trail' to 'look for him' 'because she wants to get Prince Ronald back'.

Ronald quite rightly tells her she is messy. He is angry that she is so dirty. He tells her to go away because he doesn't want to marry her.

Robbie would like to be Prince Ronald.

Leo's story
Princess Elizabeth is a 'nice' princess who plans to marry the 'bad' Prince Ronald. Prince Ronald has a tennis racquet and tennis shoes.

The dragon snatches off Prince Ronald who becomes a 'hanging upside-down Ronald, a chew-his-bum-off prince'.

Elizabeth feels 'mad' and 'yukky'. She sets out to find Prince Ronald.

The 'terrible' Prince Ronald tells Elizabeth that she looks awful. 'I'd tell her "You look dumb with your old paper bag on"'.

Leo likes Prince Ronald and would like to be like him.

Mark's story
Princess Elizabeth is a happy princess who plans to marry Prince Ronald.

The dragon burns down the castle and carries off Prince Ronald.

Elizabeth is dirty from the fire. She plans to find the dragon and 'tire him out so he just, so he just falls asleep a long time, because she wants to save Prince Ronald'. She is a 'kind, yukky princess'.

Ronald is 'not very good' He is 'stupid'. He should have thanked Elizabeth for saving him.

Mark would like to be the dragon who is the 'smartest and fiercest dragon in the whole world'.

Summary of boys' understandings

Sebastian and Robbie have little interest in the character of Elizabeth, nor in her relationship with Ronald. They both appreciate that she is cross and angry and see this in terms of her needing to get her partner back. Both position themselves as the clever prince. Neither Sebastian nor Robbie sees any problem in Elizabeth's rejection of Ronald. Leo and Mark both see Ronald as not nice, but Leo would nonetheless like to be like him. Both are aware of Elizabeth's plan to save Ronald. Both are aware of her dirtiness. Thus three of the four boys manage to turn Ronald into the central character, and the

Apart from this strong and predictable trend that the girls position themselves as the princess and the boys as the prince or the dragon, other differences one might have predicted are not there. For example, the amount of detail perceived in the individual characters and in the relationship between the characters varies as much within gender as between the genders. Both Anika and Robbie gave a great deal of insightful comment on the characters and the relationship between them (albeit from the perspective of the character they positioned themselves as).

However, it is possible to gain a more subtle insight into the individual children's understanding of the story if the children are divided not according to gender, but according to whether they understand that Elizabeth is the hero and that Ronald is not at all nice. Anika, Gabrielle, Mark and Leo position Elizabeth as the hero and focus on her plan to save Ronald. In contrast, Katy, Sebastian and Robbie position Ronald as a nice person, even a hero. For these three, Elizabeth's action is seen in terms of re-establishing her coupled state (getting her prince back) and all three think Ronald is reasonable in his request that Elizabeth clean herself up. The four who understand the feminist interpretation of the story, that is, who place Elizabeth as hero, have mothers engaged in paid work outside the home, and all of them have fathers who take a greater than usual share of domestic and nurturing activities. The three children who do not position Elizabeth as hero have mothers who do not work in the paid workforce, though Sebastian and Robbie have well-educated mothers, and fathers who take a substantial share of nurturant, domestic activity. There seems to be an interesting connection, therefore, between having a mother in paid work and being able to imagine women as active agents in the public world, and to see men as other than central in the public sphere.

This link between the capacity to understand the feminist message of the story and having a mother who works outside the home has emerged in different ways in quite different research (see, for example, Urburg, 1982; Zuckerman and Sayre, 1982; Lunneborg, 1982; and Kessler, Ashendon, Connell and Dowsett, 1982). It would be a mistake to think of this relation as a causal one. If it were, the solution to all of our problems would simply be to have all women go out to work. But going out to work is not necessarily accompanied by discursive practices in which the work the woman undertakes is seen as giving her agency or power. And certainly in the second stage of the study I found girls and boys quite committed to traditional forms of gender relations who had mothers who worked in the paid workforce.

Taking all of the children in the first and second stage of the study, the way in which *The Paper Bag Princess* was heard was as follows:

The story from the boys' point of view

The perception of Ronald at the beginning by the boys is mixed, though on balance it is positive, despite the fact that he is depicted as a self-satisfied prig. Some commented on the fact that he was a king or handsome or brave or a medal-winner. Some commented that he was a tennis player and envied his tennis outfit. Some noted that he didn't love Elizabeth. Other isolated comments were that he was a bully, shy, silly and sad.

Their perception of Elizabeth at the outset is generally positive. She is described as loving Ronald, happy, a princess with a crown, nice, good-looking and wearing beautiful clothes. But when the dragon burns the castle and seizes Ronald there is almost universal dislike of Elizabeth; certainly when asked if they liked her, none said yes. She is primarily described as having no clothes and as angry. She is also seen as sad and dirty. The boys do not, for the most part, focus on Elizabeth's dirtiness until Ronald does at the end. Their attention is more on her nakedness and this is, for them, an unspoken theme throughout the story. When Ronald rejects her for being dirty, they go along with this, but there are many clues that it is the nakedness that is the central problem. Elizabeth has thus 'turned into' a paper bag princess and is no longer the same lovely princess that she was at the beginning. Ronald does not get much mention at this point as he sails away in the distance held by the dragon by the seat of his pants. Where he is mentioned he is described as sad, upside down, and cross, though Sebastian manages still to constitute him as an agent in control of his own fate: 'I'm glad he held onto his tennis racquet so hard. When you've done that, well, you just have to hold onto your racquet tight and the dragon holds you up.'

Most of the boys demonstrate a clear understanding that Elizabeth is going to trick the dragon, saying that she is doing it in order to get Ronald back (presumably because she needs him). Only two talk in terms of her saving him. Perception of her character is unclear at this point, many not knowing what they think of her, and only three saying she is brave, one saying she is not brave, one that she is nice, and one that she is 'yukky and nice'.

Prince Ronald and Princess Elizabeth

In light of the fact that the boys understand that Elizabeth is tricking the dragon, their response to the ending where Ronald rejects Elizabeth is intriguing. Very few think Ronald behaved badly. Some of them would have liked her to get cleaned up so they could be friends again (two envisaging marriage and two a love affair); some reject her without comment, and some reject her outright and turn Ronald into a hero who didn't want to marry her anyway or who found someone else.

Those who rejected her for her dirtiness and agreed that Ronald's rejection was right said that Ronald told her to go away 'because she was yuk', 'because she's very dirty, and he doesn't want to see all that' and 'she had ash all over her'. If they were Ronald they imagine they would say things like: 'You look dumb with your old paper bag on.' Only one envisages Elizabeth replying: 'Shut up you, go away.'

65

One boy who also rejected her for her nakedness, but focused on and identified with the dragon says: 'The dragon breaked her dress ... the dragon ripped her dress.' Those who reject her for her dirtiness but who can envisage positive outcomes say that they would say, if they were Ronald, 'You're all dirty, you have to come another day and dress all nice', or, once she was clean, 'You're lovely and I adore you and you can come to my house forever', or simply, 'He'd smile, and she wouldn't be angry any more'. Of those who thought that Ronald behaved badly, three would simply ask her where her clothes were or suggest she get some, one would 'make love' to her when she cleaned up, and only one would not mention the clothes and would thank her for saving him. It is fascinating to see that the logic of gender relations and of the way one expects a story to be overrides any rational interpretation of the story. Within the logic of the story Elizabeth has not got and cannot get any clothes, and quite clearly Ronald is in danger and needs to get out quickly. It is also quite clear that Elizabeth has saved him. But what is heard is a story in which Elizabeth is in error for presenting herself to her prince dirty and naked. The story model is the frog prince (in this case princess), and she needs to get changed back into a real princess before she is acceptable. The story also has something of *Little Red Riding Hood* in it with the powerful dragon standing in for the wolf. With these narrative structures providing the basis for interpretation, the children will be anticipating that Elizabeth's actions are designed to demonstrate her goodness and virtue, and it is totally within Ronald's rights to tell her that her virtue is insufficient. In this model—which, incidentally, lies at the heart of romantic love—love is not rational but magic and uncontrollable—Elizabeth cannot be expected to use her reason to see that Ronald is not worth loving (cf. Davies, 1988b.)

The story from the girls' point of view

The girls who listened to *The Paper Bag Princess* were also mixed in their responses to the story. None of them turned Ronald into a hero, but some did manage to see him as a handsome, brave, nice prince who loves Elizabeth. The expectation that the central male will be attractive was sufficient to override the impression of Ronald as unpleasant, at least for some of them. However, some notice immediately that he does not love Elizabeth, some see him as naughty or mean, and one calls him a smarty pants. As for Elizabeth, like the boys, their image of her is positive. They see her as loving Ronald, as a beautiful, nice, happy princess. One believes that they are already married, one calls her a 'sleeping princess' and one predicts that he kisses her and she turns into a frog. When the dragon burns the castle and captures Ronald, the girls are not so obviously seized by dislike of her as were the boys. Many mention her anger, though they tend to associate anger with not feeling good. Some mention that she is burnt and some that she is sad or lost. Only a few mention her missing clothes or refer to her dirtiness. Two specifically dislike her, two mention that she no longer looks so good, and only one says she likes her. One expresses great disappointment that the clouds of smoke prevent her seeing Elizabeth's naked body. Again, none turn Ronald into a hero. He is seen as sad, angry or unlikeable, but for most he doesn't rate a mention.

Most of the girls demonstrate a clear understanding of Elizabeth's plan to save Ronald, seeing her as brave and nice, though, for some, still yukky. During the part of the story where she is tricking the dragon there is, for the girls, unlike the boys, an awareness of her anger, though only one mentions that she is clever and one says she is stupid. More girls than boys see her as saving Ronald and only two see her as 'getting him back', but some see her as having fun with the dragon, or being angry with the dragon because of her clothes, and some have no idea what she is doing or why.

At the end, some totally reject her for her dirtiness, and one for her nakedness. Some mention that they would have liked a happy ending, either marriage or friendship. Only a few think she was right to walk away, and one thinks she shouldn't have bothered to save him in the first place. Of those who think Ronald was right to reject her, the major focus is on her dirtiness, but she is also a 'bum', naughty, bad and a bitch, again evoking the feeling that she is being judged in sexual terms. Sharon (Inner City) says:

> She hasn't got any more clothes. He can see her vagina. (If she had undies on would he like her?) If she takes her pants off he might say, 'Oh good, I'm gonna climb up you'. If she takes her shirt off we'll see her bosoms. (When Ronald told her to go away and get cleaned up, what should she have done?) Cleaned her mess up.

Clearly, for most of the girls Elizabeth is to blame for the state she is in, even perhaps being at risk of being raped for it. Of the girls who wanted a marriage ending, some wanted it despite the fact that Ronald is not altogether nice and some wanted a different ending. Jane from Moore St says, 'If I were Ronald, I'd say when you get back to your castle, put one of your expensive clothes on, and tell your mother and father about it'. Joanne thinks 'they should both get dressed up'.

But most think she should do as Ronald tells her and get cleaned up. Only three reject Ronald. Elise (Lothlorien) could not comprehend why Elizabeth wanted to save him in the first place.

> (Would you like to be like the princess when she is being very clever and tricking the dragon?) I'd like to be that clever, but I wouldn't like to look like her. (What sort of a prince would you love?) None. (If you were Princess Elizabeth would

you love that prince?) No. (If the dragon smashed your castle and snatched Prince Ronald off would you bother to save him?) No. (You wouldn't, you'd just let him go?) Yeh.

Diana (Moore St) said she would not want to be a princess, since she was going to grow strong like a boy and play baseball and then grow up to be a teacher. Connie (St Michael's) said that although Elizabeth really loved Ronald, it was right to leave him. But most girls do not hear the story as a feminist story. Elizabeth is not acceptable in her dirty, naked state. Her bravery and cleverness are not powerful enough to override the romantic theme in which princesses are virtuous and clean and have no rights of their own. Nor is it comprehensible that Elizabeth does not want her prince whom she clearly loved at the outset and who could have been the key in turning her back into the beautiful princess she was at the beginning. Nor is it comprehensible that she does not accept his right to dictate her actions, and that she takes her life into her own hands. As Walkerdine notes of traditional romantic plots, 'any thought for self, any wanting, longing, desire or anger is bad' (1984:172).

The story is set up at the beginning to evoke Elizabeth as a traditional princess. In light of that image, the twist at the end when she rejects Ronald is, for adults, very funny. Many of the children are highly amused by the fact that she calls him a 'bum' but the humour for them is in unexpectedly hearing rude words in a book. The humour which most of them cannot yet hear is from the clash between the romantic frame and the feminist frame. But unfortunately most four- and five-year-olds are simply puzzled and want a different, 'proper' ending. However, the children want to hear this story over and over again. The conflict between woman as active agent and woman as romantic love object is one that engages them, and though they prefer at this stage the romantic version which fits their fantasies about male−female relations, Elizabeth is clearly a salient character who chooses, at least for the moment, to break that connection. For those who bring a feminist interpretation to the story and who support Elizabeth's line of action, this is clearly an important narrative in which the female hero makes her own choices and does not depend on a man for her happiness. For these children it is a narrative in which the female copes with her contradictory positionings and in which the usual power relations are undermined and with it the dualism that hangs on and supports those relations.

It would seem, then, that it is possible to shift the metaphors through which narratives are constructed, and to provide alternative relations of power and desire, and at the same time to relate these shifting images to the narrative structures that the children already understand. The power of the pre-existing structure of the traditional narrative to prevent a new form of narrative from being heard is ever-present, however, and there is no single solution to this for the feminist writer or for the adults who are interacting with and reading stories to children.

4 Female power

The feminist struggle against the powerlessness associated with being female has been taken up in many different ways. Kristeva (1981 and 1986a) schematises the various threads of the women's movement into three tiers and argues for the ongoing necessity of each thread, though the third thread is the one in which she is most interested and which coincides with the position adopted in this book. Moi summarises the position that Kristeva elaborates in 'Women's Time' as follows:

> It is evident that for Julia Kristeva it is not the biological sex of a person, but the subject position she or he takes up, that determines their revolutionary potential. Her views of feminist politics reflect this refusal of biologism and essentialism. The feminist struggle she argues, must be seen historically and politically as a three tiered one, which can be schematically summarized as follows:
>
> 1. Women demand access to the symbolic order. Liberal feminism. Equality.
> 2. Women reject the male symbolic order in the name of difference. Radical feminism. Femininity extolled.
> 3. (This is Kristeva's own position.) Women reject the dichotomy between masculine and feminine as metaphysical.
>
> The third position is one that has deconstructed the opposition between masculinity and femininity, and therefore necessarily challenges the very notion of identity. (Moi, 1985: 12−13)

According to Kristeva, the problems faced in deconstructing a sexist world must ultimately be resolved through work at the third tier. She conceives of this as something to be resolved within each person since the nucleus of sexism lies in the way each person has been constituted as one part of the male−female dualism. She does not envisage that this would mean that everyone would be the same. On the contrary, she imagines multiple kinds of person, each with many possible ways of being. Some of the positionings that we each take up will be masculine or feminine as we currently understand those terms, but masculinities and femininities will be recognised in all their diversity and will be located as meaningful in terms other than their relatedness to the reproductive potential of each person. The current reduction and simplification of each person into one of two types, each type taking its meaning in relation to the other type, must be transcended (Kristeva, 1986:209).

The three tiers outlined by Moi each constitute an essential and still current aspect of the feminist struggle. It is vital to gain access to the male symbolic order (eg education and legal systems) both to use and subvert it, and it is equally vital to elaborate what it means to be female independently of patriarchal narratives which reduce femaleness to an inferior way of being. Both of these remain important as long as female persons are denied access to any particular activity in the public world, and as long as their femaleness is misconstrued by those who have held and are holding women out of that public world. But these two activities, of themselves, are insufficient to bring about a non-discriminatory social order, because they can always be and are always being counteracted (Davies, 1989). It is work at the third, combined with work at the first and second tiers, that will eventually bring about significant change.

The third tier is the most personally confronting because of the extent to which identity is constituted on the basis of, and emotions organised around, the male–female dualism. The task of evolving a thought form which goes beyond this particular dualism is almost unthinkable because of its embeddedness in our own identities, and in the language and the narrative structures through which we come to know ourselves. And there is a deep level of resistance to rejecting this particular dualism, perhaps especially on the part of feminists who have necessarily engaged in the second tier of the struggle. That work at the second tier has been and remains essential. It is necessary to define and celebrate what we mean by 'female' in order to counteract the distorted definitions of femaleness that have gained currency because of male control of what constitutes knowledge. Relegating the categories to the 'metaphysical' could seem to negate that work. But all three tiers, though appearing in sequence and profoundly contradictory to one another, must have a 'parallel existence ... in the same historical time, or even ... interwoven one with the other' (Kristeva, 1986a:209).

Despite the access that women have gained to the male symbolic order, the majority of women feel quite ambivalent about power, and it is something they often claim they do not want. Power remains fundamentally contradictory to the *idea* and the idealisation of the idea of being female. Some of the work done at the second tier, the celebration of femaleness, further embeds this incompatibility

71

between femaleness and power. Women are, as Gilligan says, morally different from men, they operate within an ethic of care for others, not within a morality of rights as men do. To want power is experienced as somehow immoral, it is to behave like men, and is thus to threaten the social/moral order which is organised around the difference (cf, Haug, 1984).

Joanne sometimes revealed a struggle to be 'correctly' gendered in this way. She had learned not to want to climb up on the fort with the boys, but when new opportunities arose for acting powerfully she took them, though not without equivocation. One such occasion was when a new tree house was built at St Michael's. Joanne's intention to defend the tree house was inhibited on this occasion by the knowledge of the incompatibility between acting forcefully in public places and being female.

The day the new tree house appeared there was a hive of excited activity around it. There were those who could competently climb up the ladder and those who needed to be shown how. There was a feeling of tension and excitement in being up there as they began working out how to use this new space. There were several attempts to take possession of the tree house—including one forceful attempt on the part of some of the boys in which the teacher intervened. At one point Joanne and Tony began to control who could and could not come up. They were dropping the sawdust, which had been left by the carpenters on the floor of the tree house, onto the people who were attempting to climb up. Joanne saw me watching and she said to me, 'I'm just cleaning the floor, there's all this sawdust here'. Whether this was simply 'a story' or whether Joanne believed her description of what she was doing is not really important. What is important is that she knew the correct narrative into which her activity *should* fit. Tony, in contrast, and like the group of boys who had taken over earlier, displayed an intense and undivided attention to the task of taking over the new territory. There was no hesitation, no visible questioning about the defensibility of their strategy for establishing their territory, and no need to explain to me, therefore, that they were 'really' innocent. Although Joanne was still able to proceed with the activity there was some hesitation, some experience of doubt about the legitimacy of her forceful, dominant action. She could not be, as Tony appeared to be, fully immersed in asserting herself in this way, at least while I was watching.

It is interesting to examine Joanne's activity from the perspective of each of Kristeva's tiers. In the first tier we must defend her right to be in the tree house with the boys. At this level, girls can and should be able to do anything boys can do. In the second tier we become concerned that she has begun to behave like the boys and is not being properly female, that is, caring for and empowering others. At this level what women are, independently of patriarchy, is good, and to be celebrated. They should not have to forego their femaleness in order to be granted a place in the public world. The public world must shift to accommodate the female, since femaleness is of value in both the private and the public world. In the third tier we wish to liberate her from the tension and doubt that comes from her embeddedness in the gender order with its impositions of one form of morality for males and another for females. This does not mean that she is simply free to choose one or the other—as if there were two and only two forms of morality—but that she is free to assess her own actions in the context she finds herself in, and to act forcefully if and when that is appropriate without that implying that she has failed in achieving herself as a person. At this level, the possession of one or another set of genitals is irrelevant to the positions people take up in the everyday world.

Any social struggle, including the feminist struggle, involves the use of power. An understanding of being oppressed involves the concept of fighting against oppression. As Haug says, 'How could we even conceive of this oppression if we so unconditionally ratified feminine values?' (1984: 60).

The domestic sphere and romantic love

The only context in which women are accorded apparent legitimate power is in the domestic sphere, particularly in relation to children. As Walkerdine and Lucey (1989) show, however, this is not defined or experienced as power. Particularly in middle-class families, the mother's power is only legitimately expressed in forms of persuasion —naked power battles are taken as an indication that she has failed as a mother. Just as the mother in the episode with the three boys in the yellow raincoats showed, mothers must delicately shift and manoeuvre, they must call on the authority of the moral and social order to 'persuade' their children to behave correctly.

The image of domestic woman is intricately tied up with the romantic imagery of beauty and of love for ever. *The Paper Bag Princess* evokes this combination in its first few lines: 'Elizabeth was a beautiful princess. She lived in a castle and had expensive princess clothes. She was going to marry a prince named Ronald.' This romantic juxtaposition of love with marriage (with its implication of female domesticity) is the central subtext locating women in stories, knitting domesticity into romance as if that were an entirely un-problematic combination. The usual resolution of traditional feminine adventures and dilemmas is to achieve the safety of a home of one's own with one's prince who loves one. Walkerdine analyses this feature of stories using pre-teen girls' comic books. She compares the comic books with adolescent magazines, such as *Jackie*, which are about 'getting and keeping a man':

while pre-teen comics do not do this in any overt sense, what happens is that they engage with the construction of femininity in such a way as to prepare young girls for the fate that awaits them. How then are young girls prepared? The textual devices turn around stories which are based on classic fairy tales in most cases. They end with happy ever after solutions, mostly around the insertion of the girl into an ideal family. Meanwhile, in getting there, the girls in these stories are apparently hapless victims of circumstance, scorned, despised and hard-done-by ... The heterosexual practices of *Jackie* then offer a solution, a way out of the misery of the femininity struggled over in the pages of the comics. (Walkerdine, 1984:165)

A striking element of the children's responses to *The Paper Bag Princess* was that not many of them seemed to think that an essential element of the fantasy should be that Ronald be worth loving. On the contrary, to the extent that love and marriage are the resolution to the loss and suffering that each girl expects to go through, it is both likely and apparently acceptable that the 'prince' is the one who will cause much of that suffering. Sharon and Natasha from Inner City, for example, seemed to have an ideal of love and marriage, with a particular fascination for the traditional bride and for sexual relations between men and women, which they recognised as a central aspect of 'getting their man'. For them it was quite clear that Elizabeth should have done what she was told and thus married Ronald, though they had no concept that the husband should be likeable or even that he should love in return (though his interest in sex was presumed).

This pattern in which the woman becomes involved with a man without stopping to wonder if he is worth it is not some idiosyncrasy of these children, nor is it to do with their class background. It is one of the central elements of the romantic discourse that feminist writing and thinking and each feminist in her own practice has struggled to overcome. Alice Walker's poem on this theme illustrates this issue well:

> I love a man who is not worth
> my love.
> Did this happen to your mother?
> Did your grandmother wake up
> for no good reason
> in the middle of the night?
>
> I thought love could be controlled.
> It cannot.
> Only behaviour can be controlled.
> By biting your tongue purple
> rather than speak.
> Mauling your lips.
> Obliterating his number

Female power

too thoroughly
to be able to phone.

Love has made me sick

. . .

Whoever he is, he is not worth all this.

And I will never
unclench my teeth long enough
to tell him so.

(Walker, 1975:2−3)

The resolution of female struggle in romance and domesticity is
what *The Paper Bag Princess* is attempting to erode. The beautiful
princess who loves her prince and plans to marry him reveals that
she is also brave and witty. She rejects the prince who can love her
only if she looks beautiful and she decides to go off on her own. As
pointed out in Chapter 3, many of the children found this ending
unsatisfying—it was not the right ending, the one they had come to
expect.

In the following conversation with Anika we went beyond the
ending to see what would happen next. Anika, to my dismay, has
Elizabeth readily accept Ronald back without so much as an apology
or an explanation on his part. This is despite the fact that she sees
Elizabeth as someone with considerable independence and competence. Because contradictory discourses do not in fact preclude
each other, belief in the discourse of romance is not ruled out by the
recognition of female competence or agency, though the opportunities
for agency are often ruled out in the narratives constructed around
romantic love. This conversation took place after reading the story
and while we were looking at the pictures and re-creating the story
with the plasticine figures that we had made while talking. What I
require of Anika in this conversation is complicated, as she is not
sure whether there is some clue in the story to tell her the correct
answer to my questions, or whether it is up to her to let the
narrative continue in the direction she wants. I explain that we are
making it up, and she returns the story to its starting point with
Elizabeth re-created as the beautiful princess of romantic narratives
whom the prince loves and wants to marry:

B.D.: And so then what happens? Are you putting some mess on her face?
ANIKA: Mmm. That was soot.
B.D.: Right, and so Prince Ronald tells her that she 'looks really like a pig'. (using
Anika's words)
ANIKA: Mmm.
B.D.: And then what does she say?
ANIKA: Oh, Prince Ronald, you are a bum!
B.D.: Right, and then what happens?
ANIKA: They don't get married after all.

75

B.D.: And what's happening in this very last picture here?

ANIKA: The Paper Bag Princess is going off into the sunset ...

B.D.: What do you think she'll do after she skips off into the sunset?

ANIKA: Go home.

B.D.: To her burnt-down castle?

ANIKA: No.

B.D.: Where will she go?

ANIKA: To rent a house.

B.D.: Uh huh.

ANIKA: Until someone's built a house for her.

B.D.: Until she's got a new castle?

ANIKA: Mmm.

B.D.: And what will be the first thing she does when she gets back to her rented house?

ANIKA: Clean up the place.

B.D.: Clean up what? The new flat? Or where the castle got burnt down?

ANIKA: Mmm. Where the castle got burnt down.

B.D.: And what about cleaning herself up? Will that be important?

ANIKA: Yes.

B.D.: And will she buy new clothes?

ANIKA: Yes.

B.D.: Tell me what sort of new clothes she'll buy?

ANIKA: Princess ones.

B.D.: Princess ones? Like right back at the beginning? (surprised)

ANIKA: Mmm.

B.D.: (points) Like that?

ANIKA: Mmm.

B.D.: Uh huh, and will she grow her hair all pretty again?

ANIKA: Yes.

B.D.: And what will happen when she sees Prince Ronald in a few days after she's got all dressed up and Prince Ronald comes to visit her?

ANIKA: I don't know.

B.D.: What would you like her to say?

ANIKA: Hello.

B.D.: Mmm? (surprised)

ANIKA: Hello.

B.D.: Hello, and what will he say? What would happen here? Here's Prince Ronald, he's come to visit. She's all dressed up and pretty again and she says, 'Hello, Prince Ronald'. Ronald says, 'Hello, Elizabeth. How are you?' What does she say?

ANIKA: Good.

B.D.: She says, 'I'm good'. And he says, 'Well, you look like a real princess now!' And what does she say?

ANIKA: I don't remember.

B.D.: Remember? We're making this up!

ANIKA: I know.

B.D.: Um, what if she says, um, 'Yes, I do look like a real princess now'. And he says, 'Well then, we can get married.' And what does she say?

Anika: 'Yes, we will get married.'

B.D.: So she doesn't think he's a bum any more? (surprised)

ANIKA: (shakes head)
B.D.: Why doesn't she think he's a bum any more?
ANIKA: I don't know.
B.D.: Don't know?
ANIKA: No.
B.D.: She just thinks he's being nice now does she?
ANIKA: Yes.
B.D.: Right. OK, shall we do another story?
ANIKA: Yes.

The salience of *The Paper Bag Princess* for Anika lies not in Elizabeth's capacity to walk away, at least not in her capacity to walk away permanently. Anika likes the fact that Elizabeth confronts Ronald, and she says on several occasions that she really likes it when Elizabeth calls Ronald a bum, just as she calls her brother David a bum when he gives her a hard time. (Her mother and father she carefully points out, however, have told her that her behaviour is justified because he gives her a harder time than she gives him.)

Female sexuality

One of the primary contradictions in the process of constituting oneself as female is located in female sexuality. The children are aware that sex between men and women is part of the domestic scene. The domestic scene is one of the few contexts in which women can be regarded as virtuous. Yet any open display or even covert display of sexuality is generally regarded as incompatible with female virtue (Haug, 1984; Lees, 1986a and b). Sex is the ultimate double-edged sword. Women can use it to get what they want (for example, to be positioned as virtuous wife and mother), but through using it they can lose their virtue and thus their right of access to the safe domestic scene. Further, the way female sexuality is generally constituted makes it a critical element of the process whereby girls position themselves as object of another's gaze (Haug, 1987; Young, 1980).

The lack of legitimate agency that girls generally experience in relation to sexuality is directly related to the constitution of sexuality as an area of male domination and control (cf Mahoney, 1983). Openly sexual behaviour in boys, in contrast, is not connected with lack of virtue. It tends to be seen, rather, as a 'natural' and positive expression of sexuality, even when it is used aggressively in an attempt to control others. Walkerdine provides the following episode to illustrate this point:

> The episode begins when a girl, Annie, takes a piece of Lego to add onto a construction that she is building. Terry tries to take it away from her to use himself and she resists.

TERRY: You're a stupid cunt, Annie.
The teacher tells him tells him to stop and Sean tries to mess up another child's construction. The teacher tells him to stop.
SEAN: Get out of it Miss Baxter paxter
TERRY: Get out of it knickers Miss Baxter
SEAN: Get out of it Miss Baxter paxter
TERRY: Get out of it Miss Baxter the knickers paxter knickers, bum
SEAN: Knickers, shit, bum
MISS B: Sean, that's enough, you're being silly
SEAN: Miss Baxter knickers, show your knickers
TERRY: Miss Baxter show your bum off (they giggle)
MISS B: I think you're being very silly
TERRY: Shit Miss Baxter, shit Miss Baxter
SEAN: Miss Baxter show your knickers your bum off. Take all your clothes off. Your bra off
TERRY: Yeah, take your bum off, take your wee wee off, take you clothes your mouth off
SEAN: Take your teeth out, take your head off, take your hair off, take your bum off, Miss Baxter the paxter knickers taxter
MISS B: Sean, go and find something else to do please.

(Walkerdine, 1981:15)

Miss Baxter was gentle in her reprimand of the boys in this scene because she believed in the naturalness of their behaviour. Her failure to take serious exception to their talk is a perfect illustration of the process whereby the boys' use of aggressive sexuality is constituted as normal.

Motherhood

In contrast to the ambiguities located in female sexuality, mother-hood is almost universally regarded as a positive feature of female identity. Although it is a feature that is used against women in their attempts to gain access to the male world, it is also often an area of undisputed control in family settings.

Girls are other to that female power, to the extent that, as children, they have little power to control adults. At the same time they are, in their fantasies, able to be powerful in the way that they see women being powerful. To the extent that mothers are perceived by children as powerful, and to the extent that girls see the mother as the only powerful position to which they can legitimately make any claims while constituting themselves as female, then playing at domestic games must have a deep fascination for them.

The power that is accorded to mothers by children can appear to be quite vast. I have observed, for example, boys who are in other settings tough and dominant behave like pliant babies when their mother brings them to preschool, standing there like a rag doll while she changes their clothes, takes off their coats, puts hankies in their

78

pockets and kisses them sorrowfully goodbye. Although the male adult may be the ultimate (though often absent) authority figure, it is most often mothers who are the ever-present others who apparently rule children's lives, and who negotiate with them acceptable ways of being in and conceptualising the world (see Walkerdine and Lucey, 1989). In the following secen in the 'home corner' at St Michael's Susan takes up the position of mother. From this position it is ultimately she who decides who will be who in the game. She creates the scene in which they are to play and she finds the solutions to the conflict that arises between the boys as they vie for the position of father:

SUSAN: (dressing a dolly while two small boys struggle to put a mattress on the bed) We're driving to the restaurant. Who's going to drive? Who's the daddy?
CAEDMON: I'm the daddy (patting hands on head). I'm a boy.
JOHN: I can be the daddy.
CAEDMON: No *I am*!
SUSAN: (to John) No, you're the little boy.
EMMA: I can be the little girl.
JOHN: (to Caedmon) No I am.
CAEDMON: No, I am.
SUSAN: (to John and Emma) You're the little children. You don't go to high school. I'm the mummy and you're the daddy. (to Caedmon)
JOHN: No, I want to be the daddy.
CAEDMON: I want to.
SUSAN: (to John) You can be the big boy then.
JOHN: I'm going to be the daddy.
CAEDMON: I want to be the daddy.
SUSAN: (sits down between them) You can be the dad (to Caedmon) and you can be the uncle. (to John) (silence)
CAEDMON: I'll be the dad.
SUSAN: You can both be dads.
CAEDMON: Hey, yeah!
SUSAN: You can be a different family! (with delight, drums feet on floor with pleasure) We're on a holiday.
EMMA: We're on a holiday
SUSAN: We have a baby don't we?

But the relations between women and children are fraught with difficulties. The children, who are in some ways extraordinarily powerless, have very few legitimate ways of asserting themselves or their needs, since they rarely have the right, as adult persons do, to simply state what they consider their needs to be and have this taken as a serious statement. Women have formal power over children but very few rights associated with that. She is constrained by her idea of what it means to be a woman and her idea of what it means to be a good mother and wife. She has apparent power only, since she is captive to the discursive practices through which her femininity is established and maintained. Children have many strategies for gaining a voice in the face of their formal powerlessness. They may conform to what the adult wants, as did the three boys in the yellow raincoats, in order to be accorded legitimacy and thus a say. But just as often and perhaps more effectively they adopt strategies that are quite distressing to the adults on the receiving end of them, such as Gabrielle describes in Chapter 3 when her mother threatens to run away. These strategies may be subtle, such as clinging tightly to a female parent and whimpering, suggesting that they cannot cope without the parent; or they may be directly confrontative, such as bellowing loudly and continuously. Female parents in particular can find their children's strategies very threatening because, despite the apparent power mothers possess to insist on their own way, their unquestioned commitment to their idea of what it means to be female seriously impedes the exercise of that power. Take, for example, the following notes made following an episode observed with Catherine and her mother at St Michael's:

When I first arrived this morning I noticed Catherine clinging to her mother and her mother looking very anxious about going. Her mother was using lots of reasons with her as to why she needed to go—such as she had things she really has to do and couldn't delay any longer—but Catherine seemed to be utterly impervious to her mother's situation. Her mother explained to me that this was a very usual scene. I expressed surprise and said that I had only ever seen Catherine enjoying herself, and that when things went wrong with her she was able to think through ways to remedy the situation. I told her about the waistcoat episode. She said quite carefully that she was pleased Catherine had found ways to solve her problem—it was good if she could be assertive, but definitely not good if she was aggressive (which she seemed to think that the use of the waistcoat implied). She was very dubious about the use of male clothes to solve the problem. Quite clearly she would have preferred a more 'normal' solution. The way that Catherine could manipulate her mother to make her stay until Catherine was ready for her to go (which was when she found someone she could play with) was because of the mother's ideals and commitment to female ways of being. As mother she is committed to the well-being of her family. She takes on as her responsibility the meeting of the children's needs. In attempting to leave her child at the preschool when it is clear from her actions that she does not want to be left, the mother finds herself in a terrible bind. She believes that the preschool is good for Catherine in terms of developing her social skills, and in terms of giving them a break from each other. But she does not believe these are as important as her responsibility for meeting the emotional and developmental needs of her child. Catherine is therefore able to raise the anxiety level of her mother very easily and thus hold on to her until she has successfully made the transition to another interactive situation. (observation notes, St Michael's)

Walkerdine and Lucey (1989) elaborate in fascinating detail the way in which mothers are caught in binds of this kind. From the viewpoint of many of the girls, however, the position of mother remains a very attractive one and they spend hours acquiring the bodily and emotional competences associated with that position. Their feeding the babies, for example, was fascinating to watch. The dolly is deftly placed in a highchair, the 'food' is served out, then cooled with a circular motion of the teaspoon in the food, and the baby is given teaspoonfuls of food in easy movements from plate to mouth. Adams and Walkerdine also observe the domestic nature of girls' play as a feature in preschool children they studied:

> it was noticeable that the girls, although exploring the possibilities of the plasticine by rolling, shaping and cutting it, later brought their ideas back to a domestic situation. They acted out their fantasies, fears and concrete experiences of home life through the figures they made, but were always in control of the story line. They felt confident to explore ideas which they saw as appropriate to them and in which they saw themselves as powerful. (Adams and Walkerdine, 1986:32)

Male—female dualism in the 'home corner'

Within the preschools the 'home corner' is an area of female safety and control. Boy do occasionally play in these areas, but usually it is the smaller boys who join in and on terms dictated by the girls. They may engage in ironing, they may feed the babies when they are sitting in the highchair, and may well be called on to discipline the babies at this time, and they may engage in shared cooking, tea-making and tea-pouring. They almost never play there without the girls, except occasionally to come in and wreak havoc, or to look briefly at the things that are there to play with. If they want to play they are generally obliged to enter into the play in a way that constitutes recognisable male—female relations. Only once did I observe a boy dressed up as a woman playing wife and mother to a boy dressed up in adult male clothes and to a smaller boy who was the baby.

George was one of the few boys who openly resisted the impositions of the male—female dualism. He liked the girls and wanted to play with them. He enjoyed being in the 'home corner'. As I pointed out earlier, George did not consider femaleness to be a form of weakness; on the contrary, he used skirts and capes to give him a sense of power, and he positively loved Rita the Rescuer. On one occasion he had the 'home corner' to himself where he was able to happily play his version of father, that is, one who is dominant and powerful as well as nurturing and caring. He thus incorporated in his play the behaviours usually only available to mothers:

> George is in the 'home corner' on his own. He has the flimsy yellow butterfly cape on. He puts the lid on the kettle and puts the kettle on the stove. He goes to the highchair and says, 'I'll get the baby'. He moves

things off the highchair tray and goes and gets the teddy bear, saying gently, 'Come on, little baby, come on'. He puts the teddy in the highchair, smacking his bottom before he puts him in the chair. 'Now you sit up in your highchair and eat your breakfast, right?' He goes and gets a male coat out of the clothes cupboard, looks through at two smaller boys in the block corner, drops the coat, runs around to the block corner, kicks the blocks and says, 'Hey, stop fighting in here!' Jim shouts, 'Don't'. George kicks the blocks again and strides back towards the 'home corner'. John runs after him and hits him. He hits John back, John hits him, and George clutches his chest and groans in mock pain and walks back to the 'home corner'. He says, 'You naughty baby'. He pulls a chair out and sits beside teddy in the highchair saying, 'I'm going to give you a big brekky. You're gonna have an egg.' He puts two eggs in a bowl with a spoon, puts the bowl on the highchair tray and lifts an egg on the spoon towards the bear. He makes a squealing baby noise and the egg flies off the spoon as if the bear had flailed his arms in protest. 'You naughty baby'. This is repeated and the bowl also flies off onto the floor. George, with hands on hips, says with authority, 'I'm going to give you your soup now'. He puts his hand down with a bang on the lid of the jug, stands up and says, 'Do you want a drink?' He picks up the jug and pours a drink, at the same time saying in a baby voice, 'Nyerh'. George talks quietly to himself. He goes over to the bed, pulls the covers back and says in a gentle voice, 'I'll put the baby to bed'. He grabs the bear by the head, flings it into the bed and pulls the covers up. He picks up a jumper off the bed and says, 'I'll get the clothes tidied up'. He has a conversation on the phone and then says to a girl who comes in and stands watching, 'You're the mother and I'm the father'. He moves the highchair and she picks up a doll from the floor. George says, 'I just have to do the washing up'. He picks things up off the table and says, 'The baby won't sleep', then to the girl, 'Do the ironing? I'm really looking forward to this, cleaning up this mess.' He picks up the jumper and puts it in the chest. They happily continue ironing with a slight altercation when George asks her whether she is the (or wants an?) ironing lady and she exclaims, 'I'm doing it!' When the girl finishes ironing George says, 'Do you want a cup of tea, darling? Lovey, you like a cup of tea, love? I'll get you a cup of tea.' He goes over and gets the kettle. 'I'll get the kettle and I'll pour the tea.' She goes over to the ironing board and starts ironing. 'Darling is everything running on time. I'm going to be late for work. I have to go to work now.' He gets the man's jacket from the cupboard. He takes off the butterfly cape and starts to put the coat on. The girl walks away from the 'home corner'. When he finally gets the coat on he walks away too. The girl comes back and pours out the tea. George rushes in and says, 'I forgot my tea, eh?' He drinks his tea and says, 'Thanks a lot lovey, bye,' and rushes out. She eats her breakfast. Another girl comes in and stands hesitantly watching, then picks up a plate and says to the first girls, 'What are you eating?' 'Food.' She pours her some tea and they struggle a little over who is in charge of the teapot. They sit down to eat and George comes in. 'You've got visitors, have you?' 'Yeah, I'm having visitors.' 'I just came back from work. I just came back from work I did. Hi.' He takes his coat off and puts his butterfly cape back on. He picks up a cup and says, 'I'm thirsty'. 'I'll get you some, here.' She pours him some tea and despite her protest he fills up the teapot from the water in the kettle. A teacher comes in and tidies up a bit and says something. George says, 'Righto. There's nothing to be afraid of. It's nothing at all.' He glances at the teacher. 'Right?' (video notes, St Michael's)

In this episode George includes a wide range of behaviours in his interaction with the naughty bear. His idea of father included the gentle, nurturing behaviour typically associated with mothers as well as the authoritarian behaviour associated with fathers, though it is interesting that the baby of his fantasy is able to be naughty without any rejection from the father—goodness is not a precondition for acceptance. When the girl comes in he readily hands her the position of mother, but she is only a passive mother, doing nothing to further his game. She speaks to him cooperatively only when he establishes himself as properly male, indicating that he knows his place by going to work (see Walkerdine, 1981). This episode reminds me very much of the occasions when my older sister would get rid of my older brother when we were playing in our cubby by telling him that he was the man and that he had to go to work, thus allowing us to get on with the real business of playing with the dollies. My brother's eventual anger and violence at being so excluded was a very high price to pay for that domestic sovereignty.

Except for this one occasion the girls had control of whatever fantasy was being constructed in the 'home corner' and could dictate the terms on which George was allowed to play. He rarely seemed to be comfortable with the roles that they were prepared to allocate him, and by and large they ignored him. In the following episode, for instance, he valiantly tries to get a storyline going which the girls largely ignore, though they readily take up more usual adjacent storylines with very little prompting. The girls first ignore George, despite his dramatic scene-setting. Then a girl comes by whom they wish to exclude, and George seizes the opportunity to constitute himself as protector. He rings the police and then departs, coming back in as policeman. Again the girls ignore him, though eventually Sophie begins to take up the storyline as his helper. George then attempts to heighten his masculine positioning further by acquiring a gun, though he still tries to use it as a means of liberation rather than oppression.

> George is in the 'home corner' with three girls. He runs off. The three girls agree that they will all be mums and they choose beds for their dollies. There are only two beds and they discuss whether or not one of the dollies can sleep on the floor. One of them says, 'This is my dolly', and Sophie sings a little song about her baby.
> GEORGE: (rushing in) This is a bomb explosion!
> (He starts to wreck things. The girls go on dressing their dollies apparently unperturbed. A girl wanders by.)

CAROLINE: (with reference to the girl wandering by) Someone's coming in our house!

SOPHIE: Get out of our house!

GIRL: No!

(George rings up the police and tells them to come and get the intruder. He then goes to the dress-up cupboard, looks at the tie and then puts on the man's coat. He exits in order to re-enter as policeman.)

GEORGE: (running in and shouting) You're all set free.

(He has a big smile on his face. He then rushes out again. As before the girls notice him but do not react. One girl is on the phone, one is at the dressing-up cupboard and one is still dressing her dolly. The one at the dressing-up cupboard says, 'I'm going to school now'.)

SOPHIE: Righteo. All of you are helping the police

GIRL: (rushing in) Geoffrey and Tony are chasing us, so everyone hide.

SOPHIE: Police doesn't hide, they chase people.

(Presumably in their role as helpers, they are police too. The girl runs out. Caroline hides in the dress-up cupboard, thus taking up Geoffrey's and Tony's narrative, and continues to dress her doll. The two other girls dress up. One pours tea from the teapot, saying, 'We must have some tea'. George runs by. He goes into the principal's office and gets a toy gun which had earlier been confiscated.)

GEORGE: OK. You're all set free, put your hands up. He points the gun at the boy who has just wandered in.

GEORGE: (to boy) You are the one who is being naughty.

(to Caroline in the dressing-up cupboard) So are you. Put your hands up.

CAROLINE: No, I'm the mother. You've mucked our house up. (George makes exploding noises with the gun. He runs out and says to the children in the adjoining area, 'Ok you're all set free, put your hands up'.)

(observation notes, St Michael's)

Athough Sophie does start to take up his narrative, the scene remains relentlessly domestic with the girls in charge. Yet a mention of danger from the more conventional boys, and Caroline instantly hides in the cupboard. George gets a gun, perhaps to achieve a positioning more like Tony and Geoffrey, but his activity remains more in line with that of a hero like Rita the Rescuer, that is, as one who helps and saves. What George is up against is a division which none of his actions can undo, except when he is on his own.

Adams and Walkerdine observe of nursery, infant and junior classrooms:

> girls and boys saw each other as different, opposites, two distinct groups, that rarely, if ever, interacted. This seemed to be a very 'deep' phenomenon, and not something which could be easily gone beyond by, for example, lining up boys and girls together. For all of our recording of classroom interaction in all classrooms and at all ages, it was most common for boys and girls to sit and work in single sex groups. And the interaction between the different groups was marked by strangeness, and by excitement and violence. (Adams and Walkerdine, 1986:35)

For George, and others like him, the oppositeness clearly does not come easily. He is not opposite to the girls. He likes to take himself up in a complex mixture of what we think of as masculine and feminine positionings. But to play with the girls he had to adopt identifiably masculine behaviours in order to be daddy to their mummy, and that does not suit him at all. Neither is he interested in the way that the other boys play out their masculinity, and so he is forced to be on the margins, not recognised by any of the other children as a legitimate kind of person. I met George's father once when he come to pick George up from St Michael's. I was reading George a story at the time and he watched through a window without George realising it. I wanted to talk to him about what a special person George was, but his interest and anxiety were focused on the fact that George had been fidgeting while he listened to the story and he presumed this meant that he had not been properly attending. I assured him that George's attention was excellent, but he simply reiterated that he hadn't liked the way that he fidgeted.

Although positioning themselves in feminine ways gives girls relative control of the 'home corner', it is only powerful if they do not stray from their femininity as they did in the 'Firefighter' episode. When they have failed to be 'correctly' feminine, that is, as other to the boys who are defining their masculinity in opposition and difference from them, their domestic space gives them little protection from attack and retribution.

The school setting

In positioning themselves as feminine, girls take up a style which is in part devalued in educational settings. It is often asserted that girls start quite early to perform inadequately in school, but from the various studies on classroom interaction it is not clear to what extent girls do fall into more inadequate forms of learning, and to what extent they are just perceived as doing so. Mahoney observes that when girls do as well as boys, and she asserts that studies show that this is consistently the case, their achievement is often negated. It is 'rationalised in terms of feminine personality traits such as desire to please, passivity, obedience etc. The net effect on girls ... is the "theft" of their intellectual capacities' (1983:110; see also Clarricoates, 1979). It would seem that the further girls move away from the private sphere of the home and the further they move into public spaces (and schooling becomes more 'public' the older children get), the more their female style is discredited and negated.

Walkerdine notes a number of ways that the school system is organised to favour boys and to give them the chance to compete favourably with the girls, even to the extent of lowering the marks that boys have to achieve to be given the same chances as girls. She says that teachers perceive intellectually competent girls in terms of their unproblematic performance, displacing their academic achievement in terms of their ability to cope. It seems teachers don't see girls' competence or, if they do, feel they have to find redeeming qualities to make up for their competence, since for girls competence is eventually seen as a negative quality. In contrast, Walkerdine cites teachers' comments about boys that are glowing in their praise for intellectual competence and 'potential', and very ready to find positive excuses for less than adequate performances: 'too bright— work not challenging enough, so he's bored'. Even seriously disruptive behaviour in boys can be equated by teachers with brilliance: 'creative genius' (Adams and Walkerdine, 1986:16–17).

What is able to be assembled through these various studies of children in pre-schools and infants' classrooms is a picture of classroom life where women have formal control, and yet where that which is hegemonic is masculinity and in particular assertive, powerful, independent masculinity. What I have demonstrated here is the process through which even quite powerful girls can find themselves hesitating in the assertion of their power, turning it into domestic/female forms of action. How they position themselves as objects of another's gaze is another critical element of learning to inhibit their intentionality. I have shown, as well, the ways in which power becomes apparently legitimate for girls in domestic spaces, but that that power is only usable for the maintenance of others' well-being and always potentially able to be overridden by male force if it is done incorrectly.

It is not that female persons cannot act forcefully or powerfully, as Joanne shows. But their power is circumscribed by their own and others' ideas of what it means to be female and of the relation of that to maleness. Even where girls resist typical feminine positionings, they nonetheless learn the patterns of power and desire through which male–female relations are organised.

The romantic mythology of princes and princesses, as I showed in Chapter 3, is a potent force in the construction of feminine patterns of power and desire. It provides an imaginative vehicle through which a girl can become someone, if ony briefly, who is eventually given a place where she belongs, safe from the fearful things that happen to a woman who has no place. I have shown some of the characteristics of girls' experience that allows the romantic myth to go on being so powerful, despite their occasional experiences of power and of agency. These included the development of a sense of self as object rather than active subject, and the fragility and inhibited intentionality that go with that, combined with the fearful results that can follow the positioning of oneself as powerful, as a potential actor in the male domain. Girls will need more than new discursive practices to break this pattern. They will need to learn to want to use their bodies powerfully in self-defence, and they will need to develop a new set of metaphors that undo the potency of romantic love and replace it with something equally viable and rewarding, if not necessarily 'safe'.

5 Male power

While women have an image of attractiveness, men conventionally have a presence dependent on the promise of power they embody. (Connell, 1983:18)

Masculinity never exists by itself. It exists in relation to femininity, in the context of an over-arching structure of gender relations. (Connell, Radican and Martin, 1987:6)

In white Australian society (and many others) men are supposed to be stronger and more powerful than women. Broadly, men are supposed to have authority over women. To be 'like a girl' is to be weak, to be in danger, to have a flawed masculinity. (Connell, Radican and Martin, 1987:5)

In the development of a feminist discourse which empowers women to become other than an attractive presence or oppressed other in men's lives, masculinity has repeatedly been construed as an impoverished and negative form of being, the antithesis of what any woman would want to be. Such a construction has been used by radical feminists to celebrate being female and to enable women to assert themselves in male spheres without feeling that they have to be like a man to be effective in those spheres. At the same time it has been used very effectively to keep women out of male spheres of power by defining the very desire to be in them, to want power, as masculine and therefore, by definition, unpleasant and something that no woman in her right mind could want. In the context of such discourses it is hard to imagine anyone, even men, wanting to be masculine. Yet clearly masculinity is not all bad, and men are still very much involved in celebrating masculinity in its multiple forms. Connell resists the masculinity cringe that many man experience following an immersion in feminist discourse, saying, 'I disagree profoundly with the idea that masculinity is an impoverished character structure. It is a richness, a plenitude. The trouble is that the specific richness of hegemonic masculinity is oppressive, being

88

founded on and enforcing the subordination of women' (Connell, 1983:22).

What emerged in Chapter 3 was the extent to which the idea of powerful, dominant (hegemonic) masculinity informed the interpretation that children made of characters and of narratives, and of what they were capable of imagining in positioning themselves as male or female. One of the things that I will show in this chapter is the way in which the idea also informs the lived narratives of children's lives. One of the tasks that we need to undertake, then, is conceptually to separate out the richness and plenitude of lived masculinities from the *idea*, and the idealisation of that idea, of oppositional, oppressive, hegemonic masculinity.

Walkerdine and others construe early expressions of male power as a form of resistance to the female control that orders their lives. I will argue, in contrast, that although children occasionally resist both male and female adult power, they generally go along with it, finding ways to achieve their ends despite adult control, often achieving what they want by conforming to what the adults want them to be. The arenas in which boys practise constituting themselves as masculine (dominant and oppressive) are generally independent of powerful adults and inside a discourse different from adult–child discourse. The key element that is derived from adult and adult–child discourse, though, is the ideas of maleness and femaleness as opposite and as integral to each individual's identity. The problem is not so much resentment of actual female power, but the fact that the *idea* of what it is to be male is constructed in opposition to the idea of femaleness. This, in combination with the obligation each child experiences to be identifiably male or female, means that boys must at least in part position themselves as masculine through oppressive acts of domination and control of their environment and non-masculine others.

On occasion the children of this study, both male and female, displayed an unquestioning acceptance of adult female power, such as in discussions with Gabrielle around Benjamin and Tulip, or with Joanne in relation to whether Tony could visit when her sister was sick, or as was displayed by the boys in the yellow raincoats. Occasionally they challenged that power, or felt overwhelmed by it, as in the following episode:

Over at the climbing equipment Tony pushes Sophie and she starts to cry. The teacher suggests to Sophie that she tell Tony that she does not like to be pushed. The teacher asks Tony what happened and he refuses to reply. Joanne explains that Tony pushed Sophie. Sophie looks assertive and still a bit teary and walks off on her own. The teacher lectures Tony at some length and then leaves him. He looks very upset and sits down in the grass with his hand over his face. Joanne comes to comfort him. He refuses to respond to her and puts both his hands over his face. Joanne climbs up on the climbing frame for a while and then again attempts to talk to him. He throws himself face down on the ground. Joanne sits by him and attempts to talk. He moves his face away from her. She goes around to the other side of him and he turns his face away again. She runs over to the sandpit and says to Tony's friends, 'I just don't know what else to do. Tony is not talking to me'. They go straight over to Tony. He gets up. Brian puts his arm around Tony's shoulder and the three boys run off together. Joanne runs with them, but they head for the fort and climb up on it, and Joanne is left behind. (observation notes, St Michael's)

In this episode Joanne can be seen to be colluding with the teacher in the interest of establishing what really happened between Sophie and Tony. The combined force of Joanne and the female teacher is more than Tony can take and he comes out of his withdrawn position only in response to the boys. Of course resisting female adult power is not the prerogative of boys, though girls have a more complex relation to female power since they can position themselves as mother in their play. Walkerdine argues that girls are more successful at school than boys in the early years because such positions are available to them: .

> This success is achieved precisely because successful school performance requires them to take up such positions in pedagogic discourses. On the other hand, this is equally a site of struggle for the boys, a struggle in which they must work to redefine the situation as one in which the women and girls are powerless subjects of other discourses. (Walkerdine, 1981:23)

Teachers at preschool have some forms of power which generally remain unchallenged. One of these is the power to dictate when certain episodes or activities have come to an end and others are to begin. Morning tea time at St Michael's, for example, was signalled by the production of drinks and fruit outside in the sun and a teacher announcing 'morning tea time'. Girls would occasionally make this announcement when they saw the drinks and food being produced and this announcement led to a general movement towards the morning tea area. One morning I observed George calling out, to the girls in the 'home corner' in particular, that it was morning tea time, and it was as if he hadn't spoken. The girls went on dressing their dollies, thus refusing him access to this kind of positioning.

This can be read simply that boys are deprived of access to 'female' power, but it can also be read that that female power is seen as unimportant women's work that is not fit or appropriate for boys to take up. Boys such as George (and Oliver Button) were seen as failures to the extent that they did not dominate and control their environment in 'masculine' ways. In an interesting episode with plasticine, after a reading of *Oliver Button Is a Sissy*, Gabrielle turned Oliver Button back into a 'correct' male character by having him assert himself in relation to the bullies in the playground. She had maintained during the discussion that it was wrong of Oliver to keep on going to dancing classes and that he ought to do 'boys' things, and that the boys were right to tease him. When we came to this point in the plasticine reconstruction, Gabrielle had Oliver jump on the boys and squash them into little bits. By having Oliver fight back she is putting the world right, correcting the story by making Oliver into a 'proper' boy who can and does thoroughly defend himself.

It is already clear from descriptions of the children's play and from the responses to the stories that male power equals domination in public spaces, particularly of females but also of smaller boys. Their power relies heavily on the use of violent symbols such as guns and fire. So central were guns to several of the boys at St Michael's that their first action on arriving at the preschool each morning would be to go to the cutting-and-pasting table in order to construct a gun out of toilet rolls and cardboard boxes. These guns were usually styled around the guns in the *Voltron* series which was on television at the time. If 'real' toy guns appeared on the scene they were confiscated, but as in the 'Firefighter' episode they might be retrieved if domination was proving difficult. Where there were no facilities for making guns the means of producing them was quite ingenious. On one occasion at Moore St, for example, I noticed that the boys were using tiny candles from a birthday cake as guns. A feature of guns, of course, is that you have to have someone to shoot. This involves the problem of finding a suitable outsider, a baddie who is necessary to constitute you as goodie. The following episode captures some of these themes:

(Tony and Barry have come inside to get toilet rolls and discarded boxes from the scrapbox with which to make guns. They had been chasing another little boy.)
B.D: Barry, what are you building?
BARRY: Nothing. We're just using these in our hands.
(Evasive presumably because of the teachers' ban on guns)
B.D: What sort of guns are they? Are they any special sort of guns?
TONY: Yep, Voltron guns.
B.D: Right. And what people are you? Are you special Voltron people?
TONY: Yes. Black lion's for Barry and red lion's for me.
B.D: And who are the people you were firing at just a minute ago?
TONY: Ah, John.
B.D: And who was he in the Voltron game?
TONY: He was a baddie.
B.D: Why did you choose him?
TONY: Because we wanted to. We had to have some baddie, didn't we, Barry?
BARRY: Yes.
(Later they are discussing the fact that they need a baddie to attack. Someone suggests George, putting forward as justification the fact that he sometimes

throws sand, but the idea is rejected by Tony. At that point, a smaller boy, Simon, comes over.)

SIMON: Teacher said to play.

BARRY: (ignoring Simon but talking to the others) If they stay here they'll get wet mud on their hands.

TONY: We won't though, will we?

BARRY: No. (to Simon) Get!

TONY: Simon, off you get. George can you track Simon down if he gets lost?

SIMON: (whingeing) Teacher! Teacher! Teacher!

TONY: How could the teacher get all of us with the one of her?

SIMON: (to teacher) They won't be my friends. (then, following teacher's advice, he says to the boys) I don't like that.

TEACHER: Use your big angry voice.

(Simon swaggers back over to the sandpit with his hands on his hips, his walk an exaggerated form of the dominant boys' style. George is now playing on his own, the other boys having run off. Simon then tags after George as George runs around doing his own thing, ignoring Simon, but not telling him to go away. Meanwhile the boys' group is still looking for a baddie, and George's name is put forward again. Two of the boys run off to find him, but come back without him. They consider Simon and reject him as a possible baddie.)

BARRY: Where's that little boy Charlie?

(Charlie is an obvious baddie, being a real troublemaker, and having little idea how to relate to people, but he would probably not play at being the baddie properly and so they sit down and reconstruct and discuss the powers of their guns.)

BARRY: And this comes up and it makes that work and that comes down and they shoot off. Bang! And it goes bang into an eye, it goes bang! into a Voltron eye. (Kate, a five-year-old girl holding the hand of a crying three-year-old, Jenny, comes over to the group. Tony asks Kate why Jenny is crying. It appears Charlie has been giving her a hard time. Kate tries to persuade Tony to hold Jenny's hand as she is tired of holding it.)

BARRY: We have to find Adam.

KATE: There's Geoffrey.

BARRY: No, we're looking for Adam.

(They run off leaving Tony with Kate and Jenny. Simon is currently playing with another little boy on the tractor, looking for all the world like a typical tough boy. He joins Tony and Kate in the sandpit. They don't take any notice of him. He throws some sand.)

TONY: We don't want to play with him.

(Tony, Kate and Jenny wander off towards the now vacated tractor. Barry is still playing with his gun and he tries to bring Tony back into the Voltron game, but Tony does not take up this line of action and so Barry joins in the new grouping. Tony rubs Jenny gently on the back as they walk along. They climb onto the tractor, Tony in the driver's seat, Kate and Jenny in the back. Kate tells Jenny to sit up close and Tony says she can sit wherever she wants to. Barry has gone to find someone else.)

(observation notes, St Michael's)

Although girls are not useful for the particular kind of outsider role that was in need in this episode, they are in some sense permanent outsiders to male games, as the girls in the 'Firefighter' episode found out. This causes a dilemma for girls who want to be accepted into the boys' games.

Joanne generally found the girls dull and wanted to play with the boys. Her acceptance of me followed an occasion when she was playing alone, sliding down a wooden slide head first and on her back. I was sitting on the grass nearby taking notes. She challenged me with my presumed inability to do the kind of acrobatics she was doing on the slide. I claimed that of course I could do such things. She requested a demonstration. I said the slide was too small for me but that I definitely was not the 'sooky' kind of girl who could not do such things. But evoking a discourse in which other girls who could not do what we could do were constituted in a negative light, I convinced Joanne of my capacity and we were friends from that point on.

But acceptance of Joanne into the boy's group was sporadic. Usually she was held outside their play, despite (or perhaps because of) her high levels of competence in all the things that they did; perhaps also because of her willingness to cooperate with female adults in their decision-making. She told me she used to play *Voltron* with the boys, and that once they had allowed her to be the leader and she had loved that. But, she said, they kept insisting that she be the princess and she hated that. She said the princess was silly, though found it difficult to elaborate beyond that. Robert, the leader of the boys in the dominant group at Moore St, did oblige me with a description of the princess, however, which gives an insight into why Joanne refused to compromise herself by being the princess in order to be accepted into the boys' play:

B.D.: So is there a princess in Voltron?
ROBERT: Yes.
B.D.: What sort of a person is she?
ROBERT: She's just a lord. She's in the blue lion isn't she? To form Voltron. She's one of the legs.
B.D.: Is she any good as a character?
ROBERT: Yep, but sometimes she gets knocked off? She gets knocked off Voltron. She gets snapped off Voltron.
B.D: Is she the main hero?
ROBERT: No. 'Cause she goes, 'cause the baddies get her.
B.D.: The baddies get her, do they? And then what happens?
ROBERT: We dress up as baddies and shoot them.
B.D.: Then do you save her?
ROBERT: Yeah.
B.D.: What, do you pretend to be baddies and then save her?
ROBERT: And then the other Voltron team saves the princess.
B.D.: Oh I see, so you be the baddies and then you capture her and the other Voltron team come and save her.
ROBERT: Yeah.
B.D.: I see.

(audio transcript, Moore St)

A feature of male power here is the curious combination of male benevolence and violence that seems to be woven together as if these elements were not somehow contradictory. The dual role the *Voltron* teams played in relation to the princess is an interesting expression of this particular combination. In one of the scenes described earlier, Tony showed himself capable of being gentle and caring, but in the following scene that I observed, Tony played at being doctor to a small boy who was so terrified by his experience that he wet himself:

> Tony is manhandling a little boy in the sandpit. He pushed him around and picks him up by grabbing a fistful of his jumper. He orders him to take his jumper and then his shirt off. Joanne and another boy stand watching. The small boy looks worried but is passive like a rag doll.
> TONY: I think he's sick you know.
> (He starts to play doctor, clearly hurting him and intending to hurt him when he jabs the 'needle' into him, etc. The little boy is clutching his genitals. He has wet himself. Tony seems to lose interest. Joanne and Tony wander off together. A teacher comes over, having noticed the little boy with his clothes off. She helps him to dress and asks Tony if he knows what happened. He denies all knowledge.)

(observation notes, St Michael's)

The 'Queen of the World' episode

The vehemence of male maintenance of their power position in relation to females was something I experienced first hand in the 'Queen of the World' episode described briefly in Chapter 2. The episode began when Joanne said something to offend Tony and then deflected her error by turning attention to me and defining me as outsider, thus closing the gap between them that her insulting remark had inadvertently opened up. At first I took their mock attacks in good part, running away and dodging and laughing as they threw 'scrambled egg' all over me. Eventually I grew tired of it and wanted to stop. I decided not to pull adult rank in order to stop them. Having been given entry into their play I chose as researcher to attempt to cope with it as if I were one of them. The other boys rapidly joined in the attack. Joanne's role was a complex one since a large part of the boys' attack was a gendered one. She wanted to be one of them, victorious and powerful, and for once they weren't questioning her right to be involved. As well, it seemed to give her a lot of pleasure to have another 'girl' who was playing and who did not resort to girlish weakness, something that she expected of other girls and which she disliked.

The 'Queen of the World' episode is a long one but it is re-produced here in full, since it reveals much of the boys' thinking about and emotional commitment to domination. Interestingly, a significant part of their positioning of themselves as dominant is the use of linguistic symbols. Words and numbers are used as quite explicit weapons. They play with words, positioning themselves within the narrative structure that we create in complex and subtle ways. The competences they display would have startled Piaget who would have theorised them as locked into concrete operations at this age.

The episode was a very noisy one in which we all became deeply involved. The boundary between fantasy and reality dissolved as I actually felt the eggs landing on me and experienced the shock of being fired at and brutalised, if only with, at least in the first instance, noise and words. As Bateson observes, even though the definition of play is that it is not real, one can nevertheless experience real terror, pleasure or joy in relation to the constructed fantasy (1982:209). When I started to fight back I was genuinely defending myself, using everything that I could think of that was relevant in the children's world to do so. Some of it I drew directly from their own talk, the rest was from my own observations of children and from my own remembered childhood. In relation to the use of my own memory of how to survive as a child, I was somewhat hampered by the way in which words and rules have changed. I needed the concept of 'bar', a safe place, but knew that the children did not use that term, though I could not find what could stand in its place. This experience of involvement in the children's world is not unlike the experience of Bledsoe, reported in his article 'The World of the Cave Kid' (1977—78). In that article Bledsoe says that the world of childhood 'is rigorous and practical and yet almost mystic'. (1977—78:120). The interleaving of what adults call the real world with the powerful world of fantasy is unproblematic for these children, and for the time I was part of their world, that interleaving also became unproblematic for me. My central concern was to find a way to stop them attacking me without any status among them except my adult status, which I had temporarily put aside.

The transcript begins with Joanne and Tony and the boys discussing why there is a piece of wood attached to the climbing equipment. I am watching and describing what is happening on the tape-recorder, and standing close enough to pick up what they say with the recorder. I have divided the episode into units to facilitate the analysis of the unfolding narrative. A critical element in understanding this episode is that I was being constituted as outsider, an outsider being a baddie by definition, as Barry and Tony pointed out in an earlier conversation. The overall narrative structure is as follows:

Units 1—4   I am constituted as a baddie in relation to Joanne and Tony who are the goodies.

Unit 6   I attempt to escape into my hideout.

Units 7–10   They catch me and punish me. Others join the attack.

Units 11–14   I tire of my position as victim, escape and declare myself all powerful.

Units 15–20   They attack my position with assaults on my physical, moral and social being.

Units 21–23   I refuse to surrender, calling on magic powers to deflect their attacks. I redefine whatever they do as being to my advantage.

Units 24–26   A series of attacks and withdrawals ends in eventual withdrawal.

Unit 1   The establishment of me as outsider. Joanne and Tony use their command of language to constitute me as outsider.

1   JOANNE: I know why it's there stupid head Tony. Look, it's so children can step on it! Drrr! Dumb dumb.
2   TONY: I'm not dumb.
3   JOANNE: (to me) You're dumb.
4   B.D.:   Mmm?
5   JOANNE: You're dumb, you don't even know what exus means.
6   B.D.:   What what means?
7   TONY: Exit.
8   B.D.:   Exit, what exit means?
9   TONY AND JOANNE: Yeah.
10   B.D.:   Exit means/
11   TONY: It means get out of this house.
12   B.D.:   (laughs)
13   JOANNE: But I've got a word what exit might mean.
14   TONY: Yeah so has my dad got a exit out of
15   JOANNE: Put scrambled egg on her exit head. (laughs)
16   TONY: You've got a exit head, you've got a exit head!
17   JOANNE: Yes, we'll put a scrambled egg on her head. (laughs)
18   TONY: Yes. (both laugh)

Unit 2   I retreat from Joanne and Tony, thinking they have given me a cue to leave. I commence talking to Alice.

(Alice comes up to me and tells me that she has a skirt on.)
19   B.D.:   Yes, you have got a skirt on.

Unit 3   Playful running and chasing with lots of laughter. Use of numerical symbols to further the attack.

(There are insults and excited talk from Joanne and Tony in the background. They call out to me to come here. At this point they start running after me and putting pretend scrambled egg on my head.)
20   B.D.:   Ohhh! I don't like scrambled egg on me! (laughs) Oh yuk! Oh yuk, I've got scrambled egg all over me, oh yuk!

21 TONY: Even on your back.
22 B.D.: Errh! (laughter) I've got scrambled egg all over me, oh yuk!
         (lots of chasing and laughter)
23 TONY: I've got 86. (He throws "egg" all over me.)
24 JOANNE: I've got 29 of them. (She throws them all over me. More chasing
         and laughter.)

Unit 4 I begin to resist and to signal I am unhappy, but my position as outsider is
made clear.

25 B.D.: Oh gosh, well I'll have to get a gun and shoot you down.
         (I pick up a cardboard box off the ground and sit down, puffed out from
         ducking and dodging and running away from the "eggs". They are blowing
         raspberries on me.)
26 TONY: You can't. That's my gun. That's not for use on me.
27 B.D.: Oh what am I going to do?
28 TONY: Bang!
29 B.D.: (gasps) (More eggs are thrown accompanied by a raspberry noise.)
30 JOANNE: I've got 16, 18, 11 and 12.
31 TONY: 1 2 3 4 5 6 7 ararar . . . (counting so fast that the numbers are
         lost)
32 B.D.: Oh! the snake after me as well! what am I going to do? (Alice has a
         rubber snake. When I express alarm at her thrusting it at me she laughs.
         This is in marked contrast with Joanne and Tony who are totally immersed
         in the establishment and maintenance of their powerful positioning. For
         Alice it was still a game.)
33 B.D.: Help!
34 TONY: Nah! I've got 58, just keep throwing them.
         (raspberry noise)
35 B.D.: Am I your enemy now?
36 Tony: Yep!
37 B.D.: Oh dear, how can I get back onto your team?
38 TONY: Aah, you can't!
39 B.D.: Oh but I must be able to do something to stop being your enemy.
40 TONY: Nup.
41 ALICE: You have to run.
42 B.D.: Do I? But I don't want to run away, I don't want to be an enemy.

Unit 5 Alice switches from foe to friend.

43 ALICE: You can use my snake.
44 B.D.: What, and fight them with it?
45 ALICE: Yes.

Unit 6 The children state their power and refuse me any escape route.

46 JOANNE: Nothing hurts us.
47 B.D.: Nothing hurts you?
48 TONY: We're not allergic to anything, are we, Joanne?
49 JOANNE: Nothing can stop u-us!
50 B.D.: Alice, you dropped your bracelet there look. (inadvertently
         reverting to adult status but sustaining Alice's friendship. This is followed by

97

lots of spitting and raspberries and throwing, chasing and laughter. I climb in at the bottom of the climbing equipment.)

51 B.D.: I'm safe in here.

52 TONY: No you're not.

53 B.D.: Yes I am, I'm safe in here! This is my secret hideaway. I'm safe here, you can't get in here.

54 TONY: (shouting) No you're not!
(shouting and laughter, lots of spitting noises. The other boys have joined in.)

55 B.D.: Thank you, Alice.

56 TONY: No she doesn't.

57 B.D.: But this is my secret—I've got to have somewhere where you can't come!

58 TONY: No you can't.

59 B.D.: Yeah, everyone's got to have a secret hideaway.

60 TONY: Not us two, we're too powerful.

61 B.D.: You don't need one because you're too powerful, but I do because I'm weak. (lots of noise and throwing of eggs)

62 B.D.: A-a-argh! All over my face! Yukky!

Unit 7 More serious weapons are brought into play. I die.

63 JOANNE: You know I had some poisonous in there.

64 B.D.: Now I'm going to have to die.

65 JOANNE: (laughs) You'd better not!

66 B.D.: You don't think so? (They all talk at once about poison, other boys by now having gravitated to the edges of the game.)

67 JOANNE: You're dead.

68 B.D.: Right I'm dead. (I slump over backwards with my arms out as if dead)

69 TONY: More eggs. (raspberry noise)

Unit 8. I appeal to the moral order in defence and my appeal fails.

70 B.D.: (laughs) You don't fire at people when they're dead, Tony!

71 TONY: Yeah, but we're just covering (unclear) (more raspberry noises)

72 B.D.: What are you doing? (still attempting to be dead, but anxious about what they were doing, since I couldn't see them with my eyes shut)

73 JOANNE: Tony, what about we put some egg in her ears?

74 B.D.: Oh Joanne!

75 TONY: Yeah, put more eggs.

76 B.D.: You don't shoot people when they're down!

77 TONY: Yes you do!

78 B.D.: Why? They're already down.

79 JOANNE: (unclear)

80 B.D.: Yeah, I'm dead, I'm dead as a doornail!

81 TONY: You are not.

82 JOANNE: You're still talking. You mustn't talk when you're dead.

83 B.D.: Oh, right, Ok. (I play dead)

Male power

Unit 9 An attempt to wake me from the dead.

(More eggs and more laughter. The children climb onto the climbing frame above me.)

84   JOANNE: I've got some more eggs up here that are going to fall down on your roof.

85   B.D.: A-a-rh! yuk!

86   JOANNE: It's coming down.

87   B.D.: Oh yuk.

88   TONY: Poisonous on your eyes!

89   JOANNE: More coming down.

90   B.D.: Oh Joanne! That's enough.

91   TONY: No it's not.

92   B.D.: O-a-rh all this yukky egg in my hair.

93   TONY: Put more egg in it.

Unit 10 A trick to make me reveal I'm not dead.

94   JOANNE: This is, we all, this is gunna be good. We all, we're going away now. We're going to leave you.

95   B.D.: Are you? Leaving?

96   JOANNE: No we're not going away we're going up. (whispering)
(They're going away to throw some egg down on me. They're tricking me.)

97   JOANNE: We're going away, look.

98   B.D.: Yeah, right, I'm going to be left all alone now, I'm all sad. (silence)

99   JOANNE: Eggs coming down!

100   B.D.: Oh no! Oh help!

101   JOANNE: (squeals with delight)
(Everyone is shouting and laughing at once. Alice has all the while been standing by. She now talks to me reassuringly.)

Unit 11 Alice suggests retreat and I am held prisoner. Others are coopted as guards and the shooting begins.

102   ALICE: You can get out, you ca-an.

103   B.D.: This is supposed to be my hideaway, Alice, and they won't let it be my hideaway. (excited talk, everyone at once)

104   JOANNE: Don't let her get out that hole (to a bystander), you don't let her get out that hole and we'll keep doing things.

105   B.D.: Oh not another, another enemy! Oh no! What will I do? Three attacking me.

106   ALICE: So you gotta get out, if you want to get out you have to, if you want to get out behind him, look there, there's the way out.
(Tony is talking at the same time—it is unclear and finishes with 'Joanne'.)

107   JOANNE: You guard that door and I'll guard this door.

108   B.D.: I feel really frightened! Everybody's attacking me! Oh now I've got a hole blasted in me! Oh what shall I do?

109   TONY: You just have to put the egg on it to make it better.

110   B.D.: An egg on the hole in my body?

111   TONY: Yes.

Frogs & snails & feminist tales

112 B.D.: O-oh this is awful having all these enemies. O-o-arh! (laughter) Yukky!
113 JOANNE: (unclear) . . . the hole to put egg in it. (laughter) You shoot some holes and I'll put egg in it.
114 B.D.: Joanne you're so cruel!
115 TONY: (shouting) Bang! Bang! Bang! Bang! Bang! Bang! Bang! Bang!
116 B.D.: Oh I've got about ten holes in me.
117 TONY: Bang! Bang! (at least ten times)
118 B.D.: Oh right, I'm dead I'm dead I'm dead. O-o-orh!
119 JOANNE: (squeals with delight)
120 TONY: (unclear)

Unit 12 Another plot is hatched. They climb on top of me on the climbing frame and swing their feet close to my face. The first physical violence begins.

121 JOANNE: Get her off there. (unclear soft talk)
122 JOANNE: There's another egg on her. Put all the eggs on.
123 BARRY: Come on I'll shoot her (unclear) Bang!
124 B.D.: Oh, I think I'm coming to life again.
125 ?: You're not now!
126 B.D.: (laughs)
127 JOANNE: Bet you can't get out of that thing.
128 B.D.: Oh Tony, don't you dare fall on my face. (laughter)
129 JOANNE: Hey let's swing down upon her.
     (Someone starts to tickle me.)
130 JOANNE: Kitchy kitchy koo. She's not ticklish.
131 TONY: So am I.
132 B.D.: Are you. Don't dare fall on my face. A-a-rh! (laughter)
133 TONY: You can't shoot me—I'll shoot your eyes. (shooting sound)
134 B.D.: Oh.
135 JOANNE: He's going to shoot her eyes out.
136 B.D.: E-e-erh! (squeals of laughter) (They start jumping on me).
137 JOANNE: She's a trampoline.
138 B.D.: (laughter) Oh no!
139 JOANNE: (laughs) It's fun!
140 B.D.: Hoof!
141 JOANNE: Do you want me to do something?

Unit 13 Eventually I decide to escape.

142 B.D.: What are you up to now you wretches?
143 ?: No water's in it, no water.
144 ?: Uh-oh! (Someone has brought a pail with a bit of water in it. Several children repeat 'uh-oh'. Everyone is shouting at once.)
145 JOANNE: Come on let's stop her.
     (At this point I was feeling rather desperate to escape. I had had more than enough. I didn't know know to get out fairly or with dignity, that is, I figured a safe strategy that I had often seen them use was to run near to an adult and just stand there. Since Nancy was filming us, I figured I could run over to her, but that felt like losing, and I rejected the idea. Besides which, I didn't really know if it would work, as Nancy would have to have the power to intervene, which until now she has not done—how would she handle my problem? Instead I start to climb up to the top of the climbing

100

frame, and there is a lot of noise about this as they try to stop me, hanging onto me and dragging me down, but I keep going. By now there are half-a-dozen active attackers, all male except for Joanne. The bystanders are mostly female.)

146 B.D.: I'm still climbing, I'm still climbing.
147 JOANNE: Look what she's doing! Well we can climb too! Ha-ha-ha!
148 TONY: We're a gooder climber than you.
149 ?: Hey.
150 B.D.: Ooh.
151 TONY: Bang!
152 JOANNE: Come on, let's get some eggs squirted up here!
     Up you get and get some eggs and throw them down.
153 TONY: (screams) Bang! Bang! Bang! I helped them hold them.

Unit 14 I assert myself as powerful and agree to be queen rather than king.

154 B.D.: No, no I'm up here now, I've got power. (Luckily for me there is only room for one person at the top.)
155 TONY: I've got eggs up here now.
156 B.D.: No, nothing touches me anymore, I've got power up here.
157 TONY: Well we've got more power.
158 B.D.: No, I've got the biggest amount of power because I'm up here.
159 TONY: Yeah but/
160 B.D.: I'm up the top. I'm the King now.
161 BRIAN: Yeah, well, we've got mother power too.
162 JOANNE: If you don't think up in the kingdom of the power of God/
163 B.D.: Yeah, I'm up in the powerful kingdom, I'm the King.
164 BRIAN: Ah you're a girl!
165 TONY: You can't be a king.
166 B.D.: Yeah, I can be a king.
167 TONY: No, you can't because you're a girl.
168 B.D: Yeah! (I can be the King)
169 BRIAN: No, you can't because you're a girl.
170 B.D.: Yeah (I can be the King)
171 JOANNE: You gotta be the Queen.
172 B.D.: No, I can be the King.
173 BRIAN: Queen!
174 B.D.: This is a pretend game so I can be anything I like.
175 BRIAN: You gotta be the Queen.

Unit 15 I claim myself more powerful than they are. They use physical powers and I call on magic powers which allow me to define and control the nature of the physical world and thus to control them.

176 B.D.: All right I'm the Queen then and I'm the most powerful person in the world.
177 BRIAN: No no, you're not allowed to be.
178 B.D.: Yes I am.
179 BRIAN: We're the baddies and we/
180 B.D.: I'm up the top and I'm the most powerful person in the world.
181 JOANNE: Not like Dean Lukin (world champion weight-lifter), I don't think.
182 B.D.: I'm the most powerful person in the world!

183   JOANNE: Oh change into Dean Lukin, yes!

184   TONY: Bang! bang! da da da da da (sound of trumpet at cavalry charge) bang!

185   B.D.:   No, doesn't touch me any more, Tony.

186   TONY: Well/

187   B.D.:   I'm so powerful.
(more shouting and trumpet sounds)

188   B.D.:   Another enemy!

189   JOANNE: (shouts and then yells) Superman!

190   B.D.:   Are you my enemy too, Brian?

191   BRIAN: Yep.

192   TONY: (at same time) Yep.

193   B.D.:   Well nothing can touch me, no bullets, no scrambled eggs, nothing, I'm so powerful.

194   DAVID: No.

195   TONY: (unclear)

196   B.D.:   I'm the most powerful person in the world because I'm the highest up.

197   BRIAN: Get some water and throw it at her.

198   B.D.:   Don't you dare! (laughs)

199   DAVID: No, I'm going to put the bucket under there.

200   B.D.:   Oh well, If I'm the Queen, the most powerful person in the world, I'd like a bucket on my head. That would be my crown.

201   DAVID: Do you want me to show you my (unclear).

202   TONY: Yeah, but it'd go right over your neck as well.

203   ?:   Yeah.

204   B.D.:   He's my servant bringing my crown.

205   TONY: Oh you're not, are you, Dave.

206   DAVID: No, I'm going to (unclear).

207   JOANNE: There's a bit of water in there, there was.

208   B.D.:   Oh, thank you for my crown, Dave. (laughs)

209   DAVID: Oh! there you go, I brought you your crown. (throws it to the ground)

210   B.D.:   Oh well, I've just got a magic invisible crown on now.
JOANNE: (unclear)

211   B.D.:   I'm the Queen of all the World.

212   DAVID: Not over all of us!

213   B.D.:   Nobody can touch me.

214   DAVID: Not out of us though.

215   B.D: Oh yes I am. I can't feel Joanne's punches because I'm the Queen of the World, nothing can touch me.

216   TONY: What about that? (punch)

217   B.D.:   I can't feel Tony's punches, I'm so strong.

218   TONY: Do all of our punches at once. (punch)

219   B.D: I can't feel Joanne's punches, I'm so strong.

220   DAVID: What if I punch you in the nose?

221   B.D.:   What if you punch me in the nose? No, I wouldn't even feel that.

222   TONY: But she'd have a bleeding nose, wouldn't she, Dave?

223   DAVID: Sure! Once I had a bleeding nose!

224   B.D.:   I couldn't feel David's punch I'm so powerful.

Male power

225 TONY: Yeah, let's do it both together, Dave!
226 B.D.: I'm the Queen of the World.
227 TONY: Bang bang bang bang bang bang bang bang.

Unit 16 They try to take control by redefining me as a baby girl (robbing me of my adulthood), and as a person not worthy of their attention.

228 DAVID: You naughty girl, you're a little baby girl.
229 B.D.: No, I'm the Queen of the World.
230 DAVID: Well we're not going to play, are we, Tony?
231 TONY: We're too powerful.
232 B.D.: No, I'm more powerful than you.
233 BRIAN: You won't take anything.
234 TONY: We're not going to play with you.
235 BRIAN: You won't take anything.
236 B.D.: I'm the most powerful person, nothing can touch me.
237 BRIAN: Well we're not going to play the game.
238 TONY: Aw.
239 B.D.: Why? Why can't I be the most powerful?
240 BRIAN: Because! Then we, then then, you're so powerful.
241 DAVID: And then you win!
242 BRIAN: In the game!
243 DAVID: And then you win.
244 B.D.: I should be able to win.
245 BRIAN: And we can't do anything to you.
246 TONY: And we don't want you to win.
247 B.D.: I should be able to win.
248 BRIAN: No!
249 B.D.: Yes I should.

Unit 17 They try to take control by redefining the physical environment.

250 BRIAN: That's jail! You're sitting on top of the jail.
251 B.D.: No, I'm on the highest mountain in the world and I'm the most powerful Queen in the World.
252 BRIAN: This is higher. This is the highest.
253 TONY: But if you be the/
       (All talk at once.)
254 ALICE: (to the boys) I told on you.
255 BRIAN: I'm gonna bang!
       (All talk at once.)
256 B.D.: Nothing can touch me I'm so powerful.
       (unclear)
257 B.D.: No, nothing can touch me.

Unit 18 They attempt to defuse my power by insulting me, reducing me.

258 BRIAN: Who cares! You're a pain in the neck!
259 DAVID: Yeah, you're a pain in the neck!
260 B.D.: What a thing to say to the most powerful Queen in the World! The most powerful Queen in the World doesn't even hear these insults.
261 BRIAN: Yeah, but you're the most painful king, you can't do anything that we can.

262   B.D.:   I can do anything better than anybody.

Unit 19   The logic of my position is debated. They attempt to develop a position in which as female I cannot be more powerful than they are.

263   BRIAN: Oh yeah, what about my brother?
264   B.D.:   I'm stronger than your brother.
265   BRIAN: O-o-oh! Not my dad though!
266   B.D.:   I'm stronger than your dad.
267   TONY: I don't think so. You're a girl and he's a boy.
268   B.D.:   I'm the most powerful person in the world.
269   BRIAN: You're just tricking.
270   TONY: You're not more powerful than David's dad I don't think.
271   B.D.:   I'm more powerful than David's dad. I'm more powerful than all the dads.

Unit 20   They use age and size as indicators of inferiority.

272   BRIAN: How old are you?
273   B.D.:   I'm a hundred and forty-six.
274   BRIAN: My mum's older than that.
275   ?:   How old are you really?
276   B.D.:   A hundred and forty-six.
277   BRIAN: Well guess how old my mum is?
278   B.D.:   How old's your mum?
279   BRIAN: Twenty-three.
280   B.D.:   She's a little girl then compared to me.
281   ?:   Oh haw haw, oh yeah, well that's the point about it, when you're older you're littler, isn't it, David? That's how old you are and how tall you are and how big you are.
282   ?:   Yeah, when you're younger you're bigger and when you're older you're littler.

Unit 21   I claim magic powers and they respond with physical violence.

283   B.D.:   But sometimes you can be little and more powerful because you've got magic powers and I've got magic power.
     (All talk at once.)
284   ?:   (unclear) can't see ya.
285   B.D.:   I can see anything and everybody, Tony.
286   TONY: No you can't.
287   B.D.:   I can see everybody wherever they are even if they're down in a deep cave I can see them.
288   ?:   ya-a-a-aah! charge charge charge!
289   B.D.:   Nothing touches me, Brian.

Unit 22   Joanne gives me a playful variant of her name. They use it against me and I define it as positive.

290   JOANNE: Hi Joey head.
291   B.D.:   What did you call me, Joanne?
292   JOANNE: Joey dead. (laughs) I called her Joey dead.
293   Tony: Joanne why don't we call her ... (unclear)
294   B.D.:   Nothing touches me, Brian.
     (yelling and shouting)

Male power

295   JOANNE: (to me) Hello Joanne. (laughs)
296   BRIAN: Hello Joanne stupid.
297   B.D.:   I'm Queen Joanne Queen of all the World.
      (All shout at once about the fact that I am not Joanne.)
298   JOANNE: You're a stupid head Joanne head.
299   B.D.:   The Queen of the World doesn't hear any of these rude words.
300   JOANNE: Yes you do, dumb egg brain.
301   B.D.:   The Queen of the World doesn't hear any of these things.
302   ?:   (at same time) dumb dumb.
      (unclear shouting and talking)

Unit 23   The screaming begins as a form of violence. I resist by asserting that it doesn't hurt and redefining the screaming as a beautiful sound.

303   BRIAN: Well ha-a-a-a-a-a-a! (very loud)
304   B.D.:   Tony, have you come to be my slave up in my mountain?
305   TONY: No!
306   B.D.:   Yes you have, anyone who comes up here is now my slave!
307   TONY: No they're not! We're too powerful, aren't we?
308   B.D.:   I want powerful slaves.
309   (Piercing continuous scream—all start screaming at once.)
310   B.D.:   My slaves have to keep singing this beautiful singing, they can't go away.
311   JOANNE: Let's just leave her, let's just go away and leave her.
312   TONY: Yeah.
313   BRIAN: (Piercing scream—others join in.)
      (The screaming went on for some time and so I turned the tape-recorder off. I'm not sure how long it went on for but I'd estimate at least five minutes. They they went. I sat at the top of the frame, weak-kneed from the experience of being punched and dragged and screamed at. Before I can climb down they return.)
314   B.D.:   Are you going to scream in my ear, Joanne?
315   JOANNE: Yes.
316   B.D.:   Why would you do that to Queen Joanne, the most powerful person in the world?
317   JOANNE: Oha-a! You're calling her Queen Joanne!
318   TONY: Yeah Tarzan!!
319   JOANNE: No, she's Queen Joanne, we're calling her Joanne instead of me!
320   B.D.:   I'm Queen Joanne, the most powerful person in the world.
      (They all start screaming again so I turn off the tape-recorder.)
321   B.D.:   Are you going down, Tony, aren't you going to stay up here and be my slave?
322   TONY: No
323   JOANNE: No.
324   B.D.:   No? I need all my slaves up here to sing all these wonderful songs for me.
325   TONY: We don't like to.
326   JOANNE: Na-a-aaa.
      (Screaming starts up again momentarily.)
327   B.D.:   (speaking into recorder) Another boy is trying to get Joanne to be his friend but she pushed him off and Tony is now walking along with his arm around Joanne but the other boy is following along. Two girls have now

joined in and they've wandered off and left me alone without any apparent signal that they were going to do so. I think I should make my escape right now. I don't think I can cope with any more of this. I think when they came back up to scream they found that the screaming was getting them down as well. One of them looked a bit pale and sick when they started to scream again. As soon as I start to climb down Tony rushes over.)

328   TONY: Oh no you don't. I'm the most powerful.
329   B.D.:   (into recorder) So they're now going to try and stop me getting down and telling me that they're powerful.
330   TONY: Joanne! come here! (Joanne is running off on her own. They start to yell again.)
331   B.D.:   No, nothing touches me.

Unit 24 Serious physical violence begins and I revert to adult status.

332   B.D.:   (Brian has a sand trowel in his hand and he starts to hit my leg with it. I say in a calm, but adult voice) No, don't do that. (At the time I didn't stop to consider this, but I suppose this must have been the first time when I thought that things really were getting out of hand and that I had no choice but to switch into adult and outlaw the behaviour.)
333   TONY: Joanne!
334   B.D.:   Don't do that. That's not very nice Brian.

Unit 25   A new twist to the narrative, calling on the power of wild animals.

(Brian climbs up onto the frame, this time doing a very good imitation of a tiger or lion. Others accompany him, growling.)
335   ?:   Do you want to get down?
336   B.D.:   I can't get down. Oh well, I'd better get back up again so I can be the most powerful person in the world.
337   B.D.:   Hello, Linda. (There are several girls, especially Alice, who have watched the game with considerable concern. At one point Alice had gone and asked the teachers for help. One came over and asked if I were OK.)
338   BRIAN: I'm being a tiger.
339   B.D.:   What are you, a tiger? This powerful person loves tigers! You're my little pussy cat. (Brian is growling.)
Powerful tigers are my little pussy cats and I like my little pussy cats (stroking them on the head), nice little pussy cats!
340   Brian: You can't!
341   B.D.:   This Queen loves pussy cats. (laughter)
342   B.D.:   Lovely little pussy cats. (They go).

Unit 26   They retreat and I regroup with the girls.

(Some girls climb up beside me and tell me I can get down now. Interestingly, they tell me how strong they are and one of them tells me she has strong muscles and strong bones. At last it is morning teatime and I'm free at last. I am quite weak at the knees.)

(audio tape, St Michael's)

There are at least three lines of action/interaction going on throughout this episode. There is Alice, friend and supporter; Joanne, who is one of the boys and violent, yet interacting with me differently

than the boys do; and then there are the boys, unreservedly aggressive and violent.

Alice initiates an attack right at the beginning (32), but rapidly changes to offering me advice on how to survive the attack (41), and then offers me the snake to use against the others, which unfortunately I do not know how to take up (43). She continues in this helping, supportive role throughout (102, 106), calling the teachers to my aid (254) when she thought the situation had got out of hand. Although it was fun to attack me, she is immediately responsive to my expression of distress.

Joanne's position, in contrast, is an extremely complicated one. At no point does she assume that I cannot fend for myself. She is very excited by the game but does not lose sight of me as a person. She lets me in on the narrative they are constructing (96), she expresses interest and enthusiasm over the possibility of my becoming Dean Lukin (181), and when I assert myself as the most powerful person in the world she gives me a playful variant of her name (290−5). Although this is, apparently, not intended as a positive gift (298−300) at 319 she becomes very pleased about the exchange of names. At this point she is sitting beside me on the top of the frame, and although she continues to attack, there is a quite clear sense of comradeship between us.

For the most part Joanne appears genuinely 'one of the boys'. Her assertions of superiority over me are what initiate the episode (3−9), and these assertions are kept up as a major theme throughout the episode (for example, 46, 48, 49, 148, etc.). This is heavily interspersed with aggression. I find myself startled, and perhaps even hurt, at Joanne's unrelenting attack and I single her out for comment (114), though she is no worse than Tony. In contrast, I experienced myself quite alienated by the boys, whose attack did not in any way constitute me as subject or allow me the possibility of power or agency. I am disallowed the use of physical weapons, logic or morality, though each of these is used by them in their attack. I resort to a metphorical construction of power (that which is highest) and to the use of magic.

There is a parallel for me in this story with the narrative of *Princess Smartypants*. Ms Smartypants does not want to get married but is being forced by her father to choose a partner. She outwits all her suitors but then Prince Swashbuckle comes along and he is too smart to outwit. It looks as though Princess Smartypants is going to have to succumb to a traditional female positioning. She kisses Prince Swashbuckle. But it is a magic kiss and he turns into a warty toad and he drives fearfully away. Only through magic could she and I avoid our powerless positionings in the narratives of others.

What we were doing in this 'game' can be seen in terms of discourses of power, and in particular male and female power.

Although boys do sometimes imaginatively take up subject positions in which they are girls, as in listening to *Rita the Rescuer* or *The Princess and the Dragon,* and although girls do occasionally take up a subject position which requires being male, such as the time that Joanne was allowed to be the leader in the game of *Voltron,* for the most part their play held their gender as something that could not be altered through fantasy. As in the episode above, the game not only did not allow females to position themselves as males, but rather it was *gender relations themselves* which were *really* being negotiated through the play. The persistence in the attack and the ever-escalating violence of it were brought on precisely because I ultimately refused a discourse which made me powerless. At first I did accept the position of powerless other to be attacked, but I found this so awful and there seemed to be no way out of it other than proving my hopelessness by running to an adult (or becoming one), that I shifted the narrative that we were collectively developing to one in which not only did I have power, but I was a female who had power. Everything that they handed to me that was intended to signal my powerlessness (primarily gender), I converted into something to signify my power instead. This ploy I learned in fact from Tony, early in the game, when he showed me how guns can be defined as not for use against oneself, and the definition held because it was spoken with such certainty. Although this episode lasted for about an hour, there were girls who watched on the margins, held in thrall by the battle, occasionally overwhelmed by fear for my safety and finally jubilant and feeling powerful with me when the boys and Joanne eventually went away. More than the stories I read them, this episode seemed to open up the imaginative possibility of female strength, and it appeared to do so in a positive way, since they were very keen to talk about their own strength.

Play and fantasy are powerful mediators of reality—what is made imaginatively possible in that 'unreal' world becomes also possible in the 'real' world. The forms of discourse, the emotions and the bodily state that is required to participate in the narrative from the position of the one with power have become something that is known. These boys know well the feelings and the narratives that go with power. They are good at it and they clearly enjoy it. In a way I sympathise with their outrage at my refusal of the narrative through which that knowledge could be celebrated. I certainly did not enjoy the seemingly endless attacks that my passive (and eventually not so passive) resistance entailed, but that was far better than the position of absolute defeat which seemed to be the only other alternative that the boys were offering me.

This form of masculinity is not the only form played out by the boys in the study. Many of them adopted it in part, but were also capable of gentle and nurturing behaviour, such as that Tony displayed towards Jenny at the end of the first episode in this chapter. It is nevertheless a form of masculinity that all boys would recognise and in some ways aspire to. It is a form that requires submissive females for its adequate expression, though it can also be played out on 'feminine' or weaker males, as Tony showed when he was playing at being doctor. And although it was a minority of boys who displayed this form of masculinity to the extent that it is displayed here, it was this form of dominant masculinity that many of the children called on to interpret the stories that I read to them. In other words, even if the form of masculinity is not achievable in one's own behaviour, it constitutes both an idea and an *ideal* through which the category male and its relation to the category female will be understood.

This idea remains constant despite and partly through individual deviations, as I have shown, even when the deviation is one's own. In the following conversation with Anika, for example, she shows that despite the fact that the Paper Bag Princess is brave and that she can imagine being brave like her, the *fact* of males being brave and females not being brave remains unquestioned:

B.D.: If you were Princess Elizabeth, would you be chasing the dragon? Would you be that brave?
ANIKA: (nods)
B.D.: If I was Princess Elizabeth, would I be that brave do you think?
ANIKA: (shakes head)
B.D.: No? What about if Mummy were Princes Elizabeth, would she be that brave?
ANIKA: (shakes head)
B.D.: No? Who do you know that would be that brave?
ANIKA: Daddy.
B.D.: Daddy would be that brave, would he?
ANIKA: (nods)
B.D.: And who else?
ANIKA: David. (brother)
B.D.: Anyone else that you know?
ANIKA: (shakes head)

The male−female dualism is an *idea* with material force through which males are allocated positions in which they can act as if they are powerful. They thus become powerful both through developing a subjectivity which is organised around power and through the discursive practices which establish male power as real and legitimate. Females are allocated positions of weakness, complementary to and supportive of that power. To the extent that the dualism is taken to be true, it is true. It is taken to be true in large part because it is understood as given despite the vast amount of moment-by-moment work that visibly goes into its achievement. In the 'Queen of the World' episode I was refusing a discourse in which female equalled powerless, though I was stuck with the definition of myself as inevitably female.

Undoing the dualism thus involves, initially, a personal confrontation with the idea of maleness and femaleness that it encompasses, yet the idea is not one that is easily challenged because of the way our subjectivities are organised in terms of it, and the way the forms of discourse and the social structures hold it in place. A first step is the conceptual separation of lived masculinities from the idea, and the idealisation of that idea, of hegemonic masculinity. A second is the realisation that males and females can equally take up what have been defined as 'masculine' and 'feminine' positionings without that being a moral blot on their character. A third and vital step is the recognition of *multiple* 'masculinities' and 'feminities' most of which bear little or no relation to the genitals of the person who is taking them up.

6 Moving beyond the male—female dualism

In this chapter I want to explore *the range* of subject positionings that are taken up by the children in their play, and to look at the way these related to narrative structures and to the male—female dualism embedded in those structures. I will show how the children can be seen in their play to be positioning themselves as male or female and displaying the relevant emotional, physical and intellectual modes of being for their gender. I will go on from there to show the ways in which some children refuse or make compromises around the dualism, and will examine the implications of that inside the current social structure. From there I will examine the ways in which we might begin to think about a world in which identity is not constructed around being male or female.

I argued in Chapter 1 that we have been mistaken in assuming a apparently unproblematic relation between different elements of biological sex, and the ways that people position themselves as male or female in the everyday world. There is no necessary relation between genetic, hormonal, genital and behavioural sex, though a great deal of very poor science has been produced to convince us that they are closely, even causally, related. Even without this 'scientific' backing there is the weight of the linguistic and social structures, which are organised on the basis of the idea of two opposite sexes, thus perpetuating the reality of difference and opposition. In learning language and in learning through the use of that language to position themselves as people with recognisable identities within the existing social structures, children are necessarily involved in positioning themselves as gendered beings. In doing so, I have argued, they are doing what the scientists have tended to do—that is, they work from the appearance or labelling of genitals as male or female to the constitution of themselves as gendered beings in the everyday world.

111

A story I heard from Rebecca Kantor at Ohio State University, about a profoundly deaf preschool boy she worked with, beautifully illustrates this connection:

> Michael was four years old at the time and profoundly deaf (a sign-language-user). The children found some nail polish in their teacher's belongings and wanted to try it on. A variety of children (mostly girls) spent the next 20 minutes playing with the polish. Michael painted his nails bright red.
>
> Michael came in the next day with an angry note from his father requesting that Michael not be allowed to play with the nail polish. Michael explained to us that 'he was a good boy' and 'boys don't wear nail polish'. We agreed that boys don't wear nail polish but that some of the boys here like to try things when they play that are different, just for fun. 'No no no, I am a boy a boy a boy', he said. We agreed he was a boy but it still seemed OK to us. At this point Michael pulled down his pants, pointed to his genitals and exploded with obvious impatience, 'Here, look, I am a BOY!'

Because the words 'male' and 'female' index so much within our usual discourse, there is a lot of confusion that attends the use of the words. As Moi (1986) points out, we do not tend to distinguish between the terms as indicators, on the one hand, of particular sets of genitals or reproductive capacity, and, on the other, of subject positionings in the everyday world. She suggests we restrict the terms 'male' and 'female' to biology, and use 'masculine' and 'feminine' when we are referring to ways we position ourselves as gendered beings, at the same time recognising that that which is 'feminine' is marginalised and that which is 'masculine' is privileged. This is a useful distinction but not as simple as it may at first appear. Many aspects of being physically male or female are a result of social practice, of positioning oneself as male or female and of taking up the appropriate subjectivity (becoming masculine or feminine). And there still remains the problem of the use of such terms as 'girls' and 'boys' which encompass the biological and the social. Their constant use to refer to individual children continually draws attention to their maleness and femaleness as central features of their identity, making it seem wrong for one who is continually called male to take up 'feminine' positionings. As well, the language clouds the actual diversity of 'masculine' and 'feminine' positionings that are available, as well as the fact that these are optional positionings to be taken up and not the substance of the persons themselves.

Because of this embeddedness of the dualism in our language there is a tendency to think of males as the macho boys and females as the 'home corner' girls, and to talk about 'boys' and 'girls' as if they all somehow had those same characteristics, which they clearly do not. Any one child has access to a variety of ways of being, depending on who she/he is with, the particular context she/he is in and the discourse in which she/he is situated. The taking up of one position or another does not mean that that is who the person is— rather, it means that it is merely one of the ways in which that person is capable of positioning her/himself. Of course, with practice a preferred positioning may become relatively habitual, but it *need not* exlude other possiblities, though our beliefs about the unitary nature of the person have tended to inhibit the recognition of those possibilities. As long as the dualism is kept intact as central to personal identity, however, children will find themselves excluding 'other sex' possiblities because of their apparent incompatibility with their sex/gender.

The following conversation with Anika illustrates the way in which she generally limits herself to 'feminine' positionings despite a readily acknowledged desire to take up 'masculine' positionings. She reveals a complex and subtle understanding of gender relations and the ways in which these are created and sustained. She reveals that she is nonetheless captive to her definition of what it means to be a girl and to the fact that this excludes 'masculine' ways of being, at least in public. In this conversation I had just read her the story *Oliver Button Is a Sissy*. Despite having previously seen this story in video form, she claims she is not familiar with the term 'sissy', and suggests that Oliver should be called a tomboy, by which she means someone who is neither male nor female. She appears not to make any kind of moral judgment about tomboys or people who do not readily fit into the male—female duality. She knows Penny, mentioned in the Introduction, who, she says, falls into the tomboy category, and although she believes that girls and boys should be allowed to do what they want to do, independent of their gender category, she claims that they cannot do the 'wrong' things without friends who are also doing it. She describes the way in which the categories are so deeply embedded in her own thinking and in relation to her own being that at least in the public view of others, she is bound to act within the terms of behaviours that are defined as acceptable for her gender. In this she displays, like Robbie, the same pattern of belief in the rights and freedom of the individual, along with the obligation that individuals (herself in particular) are under to create and sustain the gender order:

1 B.D.: (reads: 'Oliver Button was called a sissy. He didn't like to do the things that boys are supposed to do.') What are boys supposed to do?
2 ANIKA: Be very rough.
3 B.D.: And what's, what's Oliver doing?
4 ANIKA: He's being like a girl.
5 B.D.: Is he? Why is that like a girl?
6 ANIKA: Because he's picking flowers.
7 B.D.: Uh huh.

113

8 ANIKA: And that's sort of, that's mainly girls'/
9 B.D.: And is that an alright thing for boys to do?
10 ANIKA: Mmmm. But it's jut not a boys' thing.
11 B.D.: Right.
[In 1—11 she shows knowledge of the gender categories, thus displaying competent social membership. She also shows (8—10) that she views the categories as not absolutely discrete.]
12 ANIKA: So I think he should be called a tomboy.
13 B.D.: Right.
14 ANIKA: Not a sissy.
15 B.D.: Right.
16 ANIKA: A tomboy.
17 (Discussion as to whether her brother David does what Oliver Button does.)
18 B.D.: So sometimes he'll do those things but mostly he doesn't.
19 ANIKA: Except he really doesn't skip. He never skips.
20 B.D.: Right. Righto, would you like it if he did?
21 ANIKA: (nods)
22 B.D.: Yep.
23 ANIKA: But I can't skip.
24 B.D.: Right. But if he could skip he might teach you how, mightn't he?
25 ANIKA: He can skip.
26 B.D.: Can he?
27 ANIKA: Yep, but he just doesn't like to do it.
[She sets up an apparently non-judgmental category, 'tomboy', in which people who behave like the other sex can be fitted (12). This is an effective strategy for maintaining the categories in the face of deviation and is not, in this sense, unlike producing the category "homosexual". She explains that categories do not dictate what one is able to do, but give one a *preference* for category-correct behaviours (18—27).]
28 B.D.: (reads: 'Oliver, said his dad, don't be such a sissy!') Why did he say that?
29 ANIKA: Because he's pretending he's a girl.
30 B.D.: Right (reads 'Go out and play baseball or football or basket ball, any kind of ball!') Why did his dad say that?
31 ANIKA: 'Cause he's doing girls' things.
32 B.D.: Mmm, and does it does that matter? Is that a problem?
33 ANIKA: Yeah.
34 B.D.: Do you think his dad thinks it's a problem?
35 ANIKA: (nods).
36 B.D.: Why do you think his dad thinks that?
37 ANIKA: Cause he, I think his dad um thinks he wants to be a tomboy.
38 B.D.: Do you think his dad might be unhappy if he wants to be a tomboy?
39 ANIKA: Mmm, cause he just wants a boy called Oliver Button.
[A boy and a tomboy are not the same thing (37—9). There is an element of unreality or pretend (29) about stepping outside the category one was assigned, in that one cannot be the other sex but one can be a tomboy and thus be other than the sex one was assigned (36—9). In this context it becomes evident that the separation of the world into 'real' and ' pretend' is an extraordinarily subtle conceptual device for maintaining this version of the social order, since apparently real behaviours which do not fit that order become part of the pretend world, that which we might imagine but which we cannot be.]

40 B.D.: (reads about Oliver Button going to dancing school) And what would you think if David (her brother) got some tap shoes and had dancing lessons. Would you like that, or would you hate it?

41 ANIKA: No, I think, I'd laugh at him.

42 B.D.: Would you? Why would you do that?

43 ANIKA: Because it's a tomboy thing.

44 B.D.: Is it?

45 ANIKA: And David's got no friends that are tomboys.

46 B.D.: Would it alright if he had friends who are tomboys?

47 ANIKA: Mmm.

48 B.D.: So why would you laugh at him?

49 ANIKA: Because it's sort of a girl's thing.

[Tomboy is a social category, not something that one can achieve on one's own without being laughed at. On one's own one simply appears to be behaving as if one were in the other category to which one does not belong.]

50 B.D.: Right, and you would feel funny about him doing a girl's thing?

51 ANIKA: Mmm, I feel, you know, funny/

52 B.D.: Feel/

53 ANIKA: Feel funny.

54 B.D.: Yeah.

55 ANIKA: And when people, when people, when the wrong kind of human being does that, I get a (pause) tickle in my brain.

65 B.D.: Do you? When/

57 ANIKA: Mmm.

58 B.D.: If a boy does a girl thing you get a tickling feeling in your brain?

59 ANIKA: Mmm

60 B.D.: And what about if a girl does a boy thing?

61 ANIKA: I get (pause) the same thing.

62 B.D.: It makes you feel really funny?

63 ANIKA: Mmm, and it makes me laugh.

64 B.D.: Does it?

65 ANIKA: Mmm, and it's like a little man is in my brain, tickling my brain.

66 B.D.: Does it feel horrible or funny?

67 ANIKA: Funny.

68 B.D.: Funny.

69 ANIKA: Like, it's like a piece of string like this tickling from side to side. (Motions as if drawing string back and forth through her brain.)

70 B.D.: And that tickling makes you laugh?

71 ANIKA: Mmm.

72 B.D.: Does it make you feel unhappy at all?

73 ANIKA: No.

[Observing the 'wrong' behaviour in terms of gender category can set up a such a feeling of dissonance within the brain that laughter is inevitable.]

74 B.D.: So, if you were to do a boy thing and that made you laugh, but you really wanted to do it and it started making you tickle and laugh, would you keep on doing it?

75 ANIKA: Oh, no.

[The feeling one has when behaving within the terms of one's assigned category is better than the feeling one has when behaving out of one's category, even then the behaviour is desirable.]

76 B.D.: No? Is the tickling enough to make you stop?

77 ANIKA: Yeah, because I'd only do it when I was practising and no girl or boy is around, no-one because they might laugh at me.

78 B.D.: And if you were just practising it alone, and um, say, like what, what would be a boy thing that you'd really like to do?

79 ANIKA: (pause) Um, fly a racing, fly an aeroplane.

80 B.D.: And if you were flying that aeroplane and you were practising it all by yourself where nobody could watch you, um, would you get tickling in your brain then?

81 ANIKA: Yeah.

82 B.D.: You would, but you wouldn't care?

83 ANIKA: No.

84 B.D.: If your mum or you dad was watching you would that matter?

85 ANIKA: Oooh, if I got a ticklish thing I wouldn't laugh.

86 B.D.: You wouldn't/

87 ANIKA: Because they might hear me.

[Achieving competent social membership does not allow one to be caught laughing at oneself. If one is observed acting out of one's category there are high demands placed on one in terms of management of self.]

88 B.D.: So you'd just go on playing the plane, flying the plane, if they were there, but you wouldn't if there were other boys or girls there?

89 ANIKA: Mmm. I mean if there were boys and girls there I still wouldn't laugh because you know I, you know . . . (pause). Let's just get on with the story.

90 B.D.: Right, OK. It's hard to explain isn't it?

91 ANIKA: Mmm, very.

Thus, for Anika the duality is a powerful force in the constitution of herself and others in the social world. She is taken to be a competent member of society precisely because she knows in this way. She can develop a set of ideals about the way one ought to be free to act outside of the categories, but she recognises just how complex this is. In particular, she recognises the importance of friends who can provide a shared discourse in which non-conventional behaviours are accepted. Again, we discussed this point in relation to *Oliver Button Is a Sissy*:

B.D.: Do you think that would happen if David wanted to be like a girl? Do you think the boys at his school would tease him?

ANIKA: (nods)

B.D.: I wonder why?

ANIKA: Don't know.

B.D.: Would the kids at preschool tease you if you wanted to be like a boy?

ANIKA: (nods)

B.D.: They would? Why would they do that?

ANIKA: I don't know.

B.D.: Would you tease somebody else if they wanted, if a girl you knew, a girl, say, Gabrielle, and she started to want to be like a boy. Would you tease her?

ANIKA: No.

B.D.: Why not?

ANIKA: Because she's my friend.
B.D.:   Your friend. What about Erica, If she started to be like a boy, would you
         tease her?
ANIKA: If she, if she was being mean I would. If she wasn't I wouldn't.

Thus, Anika recognises that 'deviants' will be acceptable if they have friends who share or at least condone their way of being, though, as she readily admits, friendships are precarious and it is only while the friendship is current that deviant behaviours will be accepted. Anika is readily able to recognise a desire to behave in 'male' ways, but she tells of an equal or stronger desire to be socially competent, something which is disrupted by the 'tickle in the brain' and the associated laughter. She has, to a large extent, then, become heteronomous. That is, she has made the dualism her own. Even alone she imagines herself being watched and has to struggle to maintain herself as socially competent. Behaving 'incorrectly' according to gender is clearly experienced as a disruption in the achievement of that competence.

Many of the children were capable of the behaviours associated with the sex they had not been ascribed, and many were not capable of the 'correct' behaviours for their own sex. Their major practice, however, is in the behaviours considered appropriate to their ascribed sex. The lack of practice combined with their *idea* of the male—female dualism meant that when they did atempt the 'incorrect' behaviours they were awkward and unconvincing. When boys played with dolls, for example, they might smack them with convincing authority, but when they came to feed them they had trouble getting them into the highchair and then the spoon with food on was as likely to go in the doll's eye or nose as in its mouth.

But children do not all take up masculinity and femininity in the same ways, nor can they limit themselves to a unitary set of behaviours that can be called 'masculine' or 'feminine'. Indeed, as children position themselves as boys or girls, as they learn how to think and to act in terms of their category membership, they encounter a multitude of contradictory possibilities. 'Masculine' and 'feminine' ways of being may overlap or run counter to possibilities opened up through discourses of, say, class or ethnicity, since each of these provides interpretive possibilities, information about how being a child or an adult is done and so on. Obvious contradictions can arise through these simultaneous memberships in multiple categories. Upper-middle-class girls, for example, may learn a discourse in which individual rights and feedoms run counter to a discourse in which their gender dictates attention to the rights of others and a negation of their own. Or a middle-class boy may have parents who are committed to pacifism and yet who send him to a school that celebrates hegemonic masculinity. How children see

117

themselves being positioned in relation to others at any one point in time, both in terms of adult–child relations and in terms of gender relations, depends on the context, the frame of reference and the interpretive/discursive possibilities known to the child and to the others with whom the child is interacting.

What follows are some of the most noticeable 'masculine' and 'feminine' positionings that I observed. Individual children were not limited to any one of these positionings, though they often had distinct perferences in the settings in which I observed them.

The rough, tough princesses

Rough, tough princesses have access to the discursive practices associated with wealth and privilege. The girls who were most noticeable in their adoption of this positioning had affluent parents, both of whom worked in high-status professions. Rough, tough princesses are able to assert themselves quite powerfully with the boys. They have access to a discourse in which freedom and in-dividuality are central and so experience themselves as having control over much of their lives. Like the princess in *The Princess and the Dragon*, they flaunt their individual wills at the expense of everyone around them. They like to be outside, to be active and powerful in their movements on swings, trees and climbing frames.

At Lothlorien the two girls who were most notable in their adoption of this style were Brigitta and Tegan. Other girls were occasionally allowed into their play and many clearly wanted to be included. They dressed in very up-market flowery, lace-trimmed Laura Ashley dresses, had beautiful faces, lithe, fit bodies and long, flowing blonde hair. Their assurance and arrogance put one in mind of teenagers rather than preschool children. But they also had runny noses, dirty stockings and sneakers or sometimes tracksuit trousers and dirty bare feet. Their fantasy games on the swings involved having giants whom they ordered to push them higher and higher. These giants, they told me, were their servants, and typically they yelled at them and called them mongrels. In the pockets of their beautiful dresses they had little dolls that were used in the elaboration of their domestic fantasies. Sometimes they enticed the boys into chasing them, but if the boys did start to chase them the confrontation could be violent.

In the following scene in the playground the boys had taken over a small hut or cubby near the swings where Brigitta and Tegan were playing. I was watching and recording my observations on the tape-recorder:

The macho boys are attacking Brigitta and Tegan. Tim is saying 'We could kill you'. The girls are keeping up a good defence. They've got the swings as their territory on which they are flying high as in a plane and they shout back, 'We could kill you with our propellor'. Tim says, 'I've got some matches at home.' Brigitta tells them that her horse will buck them off. 'Oh, he will not fuck-head', says Tim, 'we'll do you a karate punch.' The boys run off. (Observation notes, Lothlorien)

Although they were generally not interested in adult-organised activities, on one occasion they did come and listen when I was reading to some other girls. They were shy and somewhat inarticulate in that setting. They were totally uncritical of the prissy dragon in *The Princess and the Dragon,* and their response to *the Paper Bag Princess* showed a similar commitment to conventional views of femininity. They liked Elizabeth only at the beginning; they didn't really understand her plan with the dragon; and when Ronald told her to go and get cleaned up they believed she should have done as she was told, and although Ronald was not nice, she should have married him.

In terms of psychic patterns of power and desire, then, these girls are unreservedly accepting of the narrative structures which presume the power of the central male hero and the need for the princess to find her prince and marry him. At the same time they had access to the discourse of privilege and of domination of others. And they took up their freedoms associated with being a child in this particular setting, in which runny noses, noisy, boisterous confrontation and dirty clothes were seen as perfectly normal and acceptable for children. These different positionings with their apparent contradictions were not experienced as such by these children any more than their Laura Ashley dresses were seen as incompatible with scruffy sneakers and tracksuit pants.

There were two girls at St Michael's whose style was very similar to this. Their backgrounds were also very similar to those of Brigitta and Tegan, having both parents in high-status professions. They were very stylishly and expensively dressed, had runny noses, and were often dirty and set up extreme confrontations with the boys over territory, refusing to have the boys play in their game on the climbing frame. I did not observe this particular style in the working-class settings, perhaps in part because the greater adult control precluded such grubbiness and assertiveness.

The sirens

The sirens of Greek mythology were women who were able to lure men to their deaths through the beauty of their singing. The term 'siren' is typically used pejoratively of women who are alluring or seductive, meaning that their obvious sexuality is considered to be dangerous. Both the myth and current usage are part of the discursive pracitice through which women are constituted as unacceptable if they are actively sexual or appear to be so. Yet sexy women are what many men believe they want. The discursive practices through which female sexuality is constituted are riddled with contradictions. This is even more so with girls who are often positioned as seductive other to the men in their lives, and yet treated as female children who are generally assumed to be non-sexual.

Elise and Aphra from Lothlorien and Sharon, Natasha and Marilla from Inner City were girls who quite noticeably used their sexuality in powerful ways. They were able, it would seem, to ignore those elements of the discourse that constituted them as non-sexual children or that constituted female sexuality as unacceptable, and pick up on those elements of the discourse that situate sexual women as powerful. Elise and Aphra used their sexuality quite openly. It was quite usual for them to strip their clothes off and to invite the boys in the dominant group to explore their bodies. On the days when these girls came to school, the boys in the dominant group would hang around waiting for them to appear with nudges and winks, heavy with expectation and excitement. On one of the days when I was there, Aphra and Elise wandered out into the playground after having stripped off, and Aphra said to Elise quite loudly and languidly: 'I don't think I feel like a fuck today, Elise do you?'

They could control the scenes with the boys and choose how much of the boys' attention they wanted. At the same time they were actively constituting themselves as object of another's gaze, and for the moment were able to seize power because they were for these boys at this time highly prized objects.

Elise and Aphra were from well-to-do families, both with mothers running successful businesses. The teachers at Lothlorien regarded their behaviour as a natural and amusing expression of sexuality that they believed is usually unnaturally repressed or hidden in small children (see Jackson, 1982; and Leahey, 1987). Sharon, Natasha and Marilla were more subdued in expressions of their sexuality since they were constrained by what was allowable at the centre. They were able to use the teachers' ideas about the naturalness of children's bodies to strip down to their undies when playing with water outside, at which time there was a lot of excited whispering and giggling.

Elise and Aphra were not particularly interested in hearing stories, and preferred that I look through a children's book on sex with them and tell them about the different pictures and information there. However, on one occasion Aphra did sit down quietly and listen to *The Paper Bag Princess*. On this occasion she revealed a commitment to the romantic mythology surrounding male—female relations, as did the girls taking up the rough, tough princess style, with the important difference that Aphra saw Elizabeth as someone who positively enjoyed her adventures, who did not deserve to have Ronald be rude to her and who did not have to end up with Ronald. In response to the first picture she says 'I like all those hearts'. When the dragon burns the castle princess Elizabeth feels 'lost'. She has a plan to trick the dragon, but mainly she is getting him to do all these things 'because she liked it, loved it'. Prince Ronald told her to go away 'because she's in a yukky paper bag'. 'He should not have said that to her.' He is a 'yukky prince'. 'She should have run away, but she shouldn't have said bum.' (You tell me how you would like it to end.) 'Be naughty and run away to the sunset.'

Sharon, Natasha and Marilla (who had mothers in low skilled jobs) were quite clear about the link between sexuality and marriage: sexuality was what was used to entice men into marriage. If Princess Elizabeth showed Ronald her ''gina' and her 'bosoms' he would probably marry her. Like Elise and Aphra, these girls were committed to the romantic version of gender relations, but within that they did see themselves as having some power to choose.

The 'home corner' girls

For many girls their major experience before coming to preschool takes place within the domestic sphere. There the one whom they most usually encounter as carer and nurturer is their mother, or some other female person who takes her place. Their idea of being a female person is inevitably learned to a large extent through this relationship. There were several girls from each of the observed settings who took up the position of domestic nurturer. The girls described above could be seen occasionally positioning themselves in this way as well. Sweet, demure, dressed in feminine clothes, interested in dolls, in cooking and in conventional gender relations, the 'home corner' girls spent a lot of time in the 'home corner', or, where there was no suitable 'home corner', they created a little corner somewhere to play out their domestic fantasies. Their main pleasure seemed to be in dressing the dollies or in creating domestic narratives. Occasionally they seemed to extend this by becoming involved with the macho boys. They seemed to gain excitement from having the boys chase them, and although they could be persuaded to join the boys in a more egalitarian way, as in the 'Firefighter' episode at St Michael's, they rapidly retreated to being chased when the boys confronted them. The one exception to this that I observed was when Catherine donned male clothes in order to assert herself over George. Apart from these occasional digressions, the only power available in this positioning is the power that rests in being mother and in controlling domestic spaces. And of course the route to being mother is to become the beautiful princess who is chosen by the prince. Some of the 'home corner' girls' comments in relation to the princess in *The Princess and the Dragon* reveal this commitment.

The princess is supposed to be 'beautiful', 'nice', 'smiley', a 'good girl'. She is not supposed to be 'yukky', 'mean' or 'bad'. Sophie said, 'I don't want to be a yukky princess', and 'If I pulled a face like that Mummy would rouse on me'. They all prefer the dragon who becomes the sweet princess: 'I want to be a sweet princess', says one. In relation to *The Paper Bag Princess* their responses also fitted this general pattern. They loved Elizabeth at the beginning: she's 'beautiful', she's 'putting her caring on', 'she's a sweetheart', 'she loves him'. In the end, 'she should have married him 'cause he's good'. (But he's not good is he? Because he was so mean to her?) 'He's still a prince', or 'She should go away and get nice clothes on and marry him'. (Why did he say that?) 'Because she was too dirty and she was too bad, a bitch. They didn't get married after all'. (What would you say to her if you were Prince Ronald?) 'Go away', or 'I'll say you're yuk', (Was it a good ending or a bad ending?) 'Bad.' (You tell me how you would have liked it to end.) 'Stay married.'

The boys who wanted access to this style tended to see the girls not as other to their male positioning, but as good friends to play with, people who had the same interests as they did. They had to be willing to play a secondary role to the girls who were in control of these scenes, to be children or fathers who fitted in with the scenes as the girls unfolded them.

The superheroes

There was a gang of macho boys at each of the places I studied. These were the boys who had, as far as one could see, sucessfully achieved the hegemonic form of masculinity. These are the boys one generally thinks of when one says 'the boys'. Generally they roved in packs, were dedicated users of guns and were often aggressive towards girls and towards younger or weaker boys. They were undoubtedly the lords or superheroes of the playground, and always made their presence felt.

At St Michael's the dominant group of macho boys was made up of David, Adam, Brian, Barry and Tony, Their fathers were in middle-class occupations, one mother was a nurse, one a teacher and the others did not work in the paid workforce. These boys, except for Tony, I found almost impossible to distinguish from one another. Their clothes (jeans and shirts), their short-cut hairstyle, their masculine speech patterns, their aggressive play and their lack of interest in me or anyone else outside their group made them inaccessible as individuals, though fascinating to observe as a group. They were very impatient with the stories, and on one occasion when I did get them to sit down and listen, David said very impatiently to the teacher as she walked by, 'Do we have to do this?' It was as if listening to stories positioned them as child which was not what they were into while at preschool and with each other.

At Lothlorien the macho gang was made up of Tim, Chris, Tony and Larry. As at St Michael's, they were hard to get near and it was not possible to get to know them as individuals. All four had both parents working at high-status jobs. The major features that distinguished them from the St Michael's gang were that they had watches, which seemed to be some sort of status symbol, they fought with each other rather than finding outsiders to fight, they displayed extreme interest in the sirens, and when they were roving around the playground, they usually had their school satchels on their backs, which made them look as if they were adventurers going off into the wild. A not atypical event recorded in the 'block room' was as follows:

'The construction with blocks has degenerated into kicking and fighting. "Idiot!" "Fuckwit!" "I'm going to get you!" "No you're not, shit!" "I've got a big hurt on the chin!" "Stupid!"' (observation notes, Lothlorien). For the fleeting moments when I did get them to sit down and listen, their comments were brief and revealed a predictably negative attitude to females, with the one exception of *Rita the Rescuer*, whom Tony said he would like to be like. As for the Paper Bag Princess, however, she had obviously decided that they weren't going to get married any more 'because she was a bum'. They said they didn't know why she did what she did, but 'she should be hit'.

The macho boys at Inner City were Sunil, Tan and Velimir. They seemed a bit scatty and mindless and stirred a lot of trouble with the girls by wrecking their jigsaws, picking up things they were playing with and throwing them down. I did not have much success in reading them stories as their English was not really good enough to follow the stories in detail or to discuss the ideas that they may have had.

At Moore St the macho group was much like the other groups, though they had a marked leader who organised their play through his superior linguistic skills and his knowledge of the environment. His control was more through the intellect than brute force, but it was decided control nonetheless.

Joanne was the only girl who adopted this style. She did not want the boys to accept her as if she were the kind of girl that they took girls to be. She wanted them to accept her as someone who had the same rights, interests, skills, capabilities and interests as they did, though she did not want them to pretend she was a boy. She was keen that people recognise her as a female, though she had little interest in 'feminine' activities and gained little pleasure from the company of girls. She was much happier when her mother was at work and would come and tell me on the days when her mother was working. She wanted gender to be irrelevant so she could get on with what she wanted to do, but found herself excluded or put in positions that she did not want (such as the princess in *Voltron*), simply on the grounds that she was female, her sex being made relevant when she could not see its relevance. The continual compromises that she made in order to be accepted by the boys made it very hard for her to support unequivocally Elizabeth's action at the end. At first, 'She is a pretty princess' 'who loves boys'. She observed of Ronald, 'I bet he doesn't want to marry her ...' 'cause he's not a very good boy and he's not even going to talk to her ... He's turned around ... and he's not even talking to her.' She still liked Elizabeth after her castle was burned, though noted that she was not as pretty. She understood Elizabeth's anger with the dragon and her plan to 'get that boy back'. In the end Ronald told her to go away 'Because she was too dirty'. (Do you think he should have said that?) 'No, they should both get dressed up.' (What would you have said if you'd been Ronald?) 'I wouldn't say [pause] I don't know.' (Would you have been pleased that she had come to save you?) 'No, I just would, I just would, I just wouldn't even talk to her.' (Why not?) 'Because, I don't [pause] nothing.' (Would you run out of the cave?) 'Nuh uh,' (How does Elizabeth feel?) 'I don't [pause] angry.' (Did you like that story?) 'Mmm'.

The articulate intellectuals

Life for boys who adopted this style was not at all straightforward. As Connell et al. point out, the dominant superhero style described above is what masculinity is supposed to be about. Those boys or men who do not position themselves in this way experience an inevitable tension in relation to their masculinity:

> To 'be a man' is to show the qualities needed to sustain power—courage in the face of threat or conflict define an admired, socially dominant form of masculinity. But this does not settle the everyday reality of men's lives, for most men can't or won't live according to the ideal pattern. Rather it defines a basic *tension* in masculinity. (Connell, Radican and Martin, 1987:5)

Oliver Button Is a Sissy is an attempt to provide a way of thinking about non-hegemonic masculinity that makes it acceptable. As I have shown, this is an extremely difficult thing to do. The plight of

124

tne boys who can't or won't adopt the style of hegemonic masculinity is that life is complex and filled with tension. Many attempt to alleviate that tension by acquiring some of the competences associated with hegemonic masculinity so that their maleness is not cast in doubt, thus freeing them to pursue their less masculine interests.

There were several boys in each of the settings studied who could be described as 'sensitive and articulate'. The majority were from middle-class or upper-middle-class backgrounds, though George's father was a blue-collar worker. Generally, the boys who attempted to be both acceptable to the macho boys and articulate and sensitive had mothers who worked in the paid workforce. Interestingly, those who appeared to make no gestures towards positioning themselves in hegemonic forms of masculinity and who were, for the most part, articulate and sensitive had mothers who did not work in the paid workforce.

The boys who adopt this style are generally delightful to talk to. They talk with ease about a wide range of topics and clearly enjoy doing so. Essentially these boys see themselves as masculine, but their idea of masculinity encompasses many of the behaviours which are excluded by the boys who predominantly adopt the macho style, at least for the period while they adopt it. As well, their major interest in girls is in terms of friendship with them rather than sexual/romantic relationships. Tony, who was accepted as one of the macho boys but who also enjoyed his friendship with Joanne, was often torn between the two. Occasionally the boys rejected him because of his 'feminine' interests. His mother told me that he blamed this rejection on Joanne, but he was nevertheless continually drawn to her. It is possible that some of his more gross displays of masculinity were a desperate attempt to ensure the continuing acceptance of the boys. In relation to Princess Elizabeth's adventures with the dragon, he says:

TONY: She's going to find Prince Ronald. She's going to ask the dragon to blow the fire.
B.D.: What sort of a girl does that make her?
TONY: A happy girl.
B.D.: What do you think she is going to do?
TONY: She's going to untie him.
B.D.: Why?
TONY: Because he needs help . . .
B.D.: Do you think Prince Ronald should have said that?
TONY: (nods)
B.D.: Why?
TONY: Because, um, because princesses should wear nice clothes. I'd say go and put your clothes on [politely].
B.D.: Would you have like them to get married?
TONY: No.

125

B.D.: What would you have liked?
TONY: Oh, I think she just loved him.
B.D.: If she came back the next day all dressed up like a princess, what would happen then?
TONY: He'll smile.
B.D.: And would they be friends again?
TONY: Yeah.
B.D.: And do you think she'll still be angry because he was rude to her?
TONY: No.

There were of course, many girls who adopted this style. Anika, for example, was more than happy to sit for hours discussing the complex problems surrounding gender. She liked to hear the stories that dealt with adult conflicts as well, such as *A Fortunate Catastrophe* and *Arthur and Clementine*. The observations she produced in relation to these revealed the same intricate forms of analysis that she provided in the 'tickle-in-the-brain' conversation, discussed at the beginning of this chapter. But as I have observed earlier, this did not let her off the hook of romantic notions of male–female relations nor of her own boundedness within female genderedness. Girls who adopt this style may have to make the kinds of compromises suggested by Rita the Rescuer—that is, they can assert themselves but only for other people's benefit, not for their own benefit nor for their own glorification. Otherwise they will open themselves up to accusations of being male, of being immoral, 'incorrect' and definitely not female.

Some forms of 'masculinity' and 'femininity' are 'safe'. If correctly achieved, they are recognised as high-status ways of being. The children who achieve them are popular and other children aspire to be in their group. The superhero boys, the 'home corner' girls, the rough, tough princesses and the sirens have adopted the major 'safe' forms. These forms fall clearly within the poles of gender and do not overlap or undermine the sense of oppositeness. They leave intact the power relations between men and women, these being imaginatively constructed around ideas of romantic love on the one hand and dominance and control on the other. Within each of the polar opposites there are identifiable powers and rewards. One may be denied access to the male arena as a domestic nurturant girl, but there are compensations: there are safe places to be in which there are clearly defined and fascinating activities (dressing dollies can be incredibly absorbing), and you can have excitement if you want it by getting the boys to chase you, and even (if you are a rough, tough princess) confronting them during the chase. Similarly with the macho boys, their relations with each other and with the girls are clear and there are multiple symbols of successful masculinity to be wielded. They have a sense of power, competence, hardness—their bodies are filled with a good feeling of strength and well-being, and they have the capacity to deal with all-comers. ('How could the teacher get all of us with the one of her?' Tony scathingly asks of Simon when Simon thinks that enlisting the teacher's aid will gain him entry into the boys' group.)

If you successfully adopt one of these styles, you've made it. Rough, tough princesses and sirens are higher status than the 'home corner' girls, and their life is somewhat more exciting since it holds the possibility of sometimes getting the better of the boys. All are nonetheless unequivocally 'feminine' and are preparing the ground for some variant of oppressive gender relations. These children have made the accommodations required of them and are able to make gender relations appear fairly natural, and the tension, opposition and excitement seem an inevitable form of gender relations.

For some few children, the opposition and incompatibility of 'masculine' and 'feminine' positionings did not seem to arise. Mark, whose father plays a genuinely equal part at home with Mark's mother, was one of the few boys who seemed equally comfortable with 'masculine' and 'feminine' positionings. In listening to *Oliver Button Is a Sissy*, he was absolutely clear about Oliver's rights. He referred to his own experience of girls' things to justify this. He said, 'I do lots of things that girls do and lots of things that boys do. Like my dad bought me a She Ra, and I like skipping and stuff and also I'd like to get the castle that She Ra lives in, and stuff like that ... I feel happy doing girls' things, and after all I do go to dance.' He did, however, express annoyance with his father for talking about his dancing class, and a lot of negotiation was involved over incidents where he rejected things 'feminine' and showed inordinate preference for 'masculine' style.

Daniel at Inner City had a similar attitude, which he explained when we were talking about Oliver Button. He thought that Oliver's problem was that he went to dancing class *every* day (although that is not what Oliver actually did). Daniel only went to ballet a couple of days a week and that, he said, is less likely to cause rejection by the other boys. Daniel, like Mark, had a mother who worked in the paid workforce, and his parents, unusually for Inner City, had high-status professions. Daniel appeared not to be at all bothered by the idea that boys might do the things that girls do: he seemed comfortable with the idea that he was biologically male and that he could take up 'feminine' positions. In the following conversation I was trying to explain the world 'sissy', because he said he didn't know that it meant:

B.D.: Well, Oliver Button is a boy who likes to do things that usually girls do and people be really mean to him. Some people be really mean to him and call him a sissy. 'Cause that's a word they think that you should call people who do girl things. OK?
DANIEL: I actually do boy things and half girl things.

127

B.D.:   Do you, Daniel?
DANIEL: Yeah.
B.D.:   I do too. I do some boy things and some girl things.
DANIEL: I do half of them.

For yet others their assigned gender category is a straitjacket they have a lot of trouble wearing. In stepping outside what is viewed as 'correct' behaviour, they suffer continually as they experience the category-maintenance work that their 'deviance' gives rise to. Their resistance is the source of a lot of conflict, or, in the case of Daniel and Mark, a lot of work on the part of their parents to help them negotiate their unboundedness. The two children, who were observably most confronted in terms of the ways they wanted to be and the constraints of their gender, were at pains to point out that they were capable of positioning themselves 'correctly' in terms of their gender, making greater claims in this direction than their observed behaviour would seem to warrant. This suggests that they experienced considerable tension between the way that they knew they ought to be and the way they actually were (see Walkerdine, 1985). George and Joanne in their responses to *Oliver Button Is a Sissy* reveal this dilemma quite clearly:

1   B.D.:   (reading) Oliver Button was called a sissy. He didn't like to do the things that boys are supposed to do. What are boys supposed to do?
2   JOANNE: Play football, and he doesn't like playing football.
3   B.D.:   (reads about Oliver liking to skip) Do you like to skip?
4   JOANNE: Yep. I skip a lot. I don't even stop skipping.
5   B.D.:   Uh huh. (reads about Oliver liking to 'put on costumes') Do you like to put on costumes? Would you like to put on costumes?
6   JOANNE: No. But I like to be Ellie's mother.
7   B.D.:   Who's Ellie?
8   JOANNE: My baby sister.
9   B.D.:   Uh huh. (reads about Oliver's dad begging him to go out and play ball) Why did his dad say that?
10   JOANNE: 'Cause he's a boy.
11   B.D.:   And did his dad think that he should do boy things? Do all dads think that, that boys should do boys' things and that girls should do girls' things?
12   JOANNE: Uh huh.
13   B.D.:   They do?
14   JOANNE: My dad, my dad just lets me do anything.
15   B.D.:   Does he? Are you allowed to do boy things as well as girl things?
16   JOANNE: No I didn't, I don't like, I like playing boys' things too.
17   B.D.:   Yeah.
18   JOANNE: 'Cause I play (unclear) and I'm a boy in that.
19   B.D.:   Yeah. And your dad doesn't mind?
20   JOANNE: Yeah.
21   B.D.:   And what about your mum? Does she mind?
22   JOANNE: No. . . .
23   B.D.:   So how does Oliver feel?

24 JOANNE: Not very good. He wants to be on the boy team.
25 B.D.: But he doesn't want to do what the boys do, does he?
26 JOANNE: Mmm.
27 B.D.: So what should he do?
28 JOANNE: He should have to do the boys' things . . .
29 B.D.: (reads about the boys crossing out 'sissy' and writing 'star') So why had they done that?
30 JOANNE: 'Cause they like him now and they're not going to tease him, and they're going to play with him.
31 B.D.: Right. So they like him now because he's . . . what?
32 JOANNE: He's a sissy and he's a star.
33 B.D.: Right. And they don't mind any more?
34 JOANNE: No.
35 B.D.: Right, right. So do you ever want to do things, tell me what boy things you do?
36 JOANNE: I don't do any boy things. I just be Ellie's mother and play with Ellie and play with my new Barbie stuff and everything.
37 B.D.: What sort of, but what sort of, don't you like to any boy things?
38 JOANNE: (shakes head)
39 B.D.: No? So you just want to do girl things?
40 JOANNE: Uh huh.
41 B.D.: So why do you mostly have boys for friends instead of girls?
42 JOANNE: Oh, I've got girl and boy friends.
43 B.D.: Have you? And which ones do you like to be with the most?
44 JOANNE: Boys. I like boys very much.
45 B.D.: Do you? So why do you like to be with the boys?
46 JOANNE: Because I like them very much.
47 B.D.: The boys, or do you like the things the boys do?
48 JOANNE: I like the boys better than the girls.
49 B.D.: Do you?
50 JOANNE: But I still like the girls, but . . .

Joanne's conflict is evident throughout this conversation. She is torn between providing proof that she knows how to be a girl (4, 6, 36, 38) and the fact that she prefers to do boys' things (16, 18, 44). She empathises with Oliver (2, 24) and yet thinks he should learn how to behave 'correctly' according to his gender (11–12, 28) assuming, that, like her, Oliver is unhappy because he wants to be on 'the boys' team' (24). She is very wary of saying that she straightforwardly prefers boys' things (16) and ends by denying that she likes boys' things at all (36), this being the ultimate proof that she needs to establish that she has 'correctly' positioned herself as a girl. The only legitimate explanation that she can find for her preference for the boys is her caring for them (44, 46, 48). She cannot, within a discussion about her genderedness, put herself forward as preferring the behaviours in and for themselves, since this will call into question her understanding of the way the categories work as well as her success as a gendered person. Because 'boyness' is the opposite of 'girlness' she cannot be a girl who prefers boys' things since that

129

involves an impossible denial of the meaning of the categories themselves. Thus, her love of boys' activities cannot be celebrated and is converted into a liking for the people who can legitimately have access to the things that she herself wants to do.

George's response to Oliver Button shows the same kind of dilemma. At first he happily claims that he likes to do the things that boys are not 'supposed to do', but as the discussion progresses he reveals that he is aware that there are category boundaries and that ultimately adult men have the right/ability to declare exactly what these boundaries are and thus to declare George (and me) in the wrong:

1 B.D.: (reads about Oliver being a sissy) What are boys supposed to do?
2 GEORGE: Pick flowers with their mother.
3 B.D.: Well he [Oliver] likes to pick flowers. But this story is saying that boys are supposed to play football and that sort of thing.
4 GEORGE: Yeah.
5 B.D.: Yeah, and do you think boys are supposed to pick flowers with their mum?
6 GEORGE: Uh huh ...
7 B.D.: And do you like to sing and dance?
8 GEORGE: Yup.
9 B.D.: Yup. (reads) Now why did his dad say that?
10 GEORGE: Because he's a boy.
11 B.D.: And are boys supposed to go outside and play football?
12 GEORGE: Yep.
13 B.D.: And do you think that his dad thinks that it matters? Is there something wrong with doing these other things?
14 GEORGE: Yep.
15 B.D.: Why does his dad think that?
16 GEORGE: Because he thinks he's going to be a girl.
17 B.D.: Oh. Do you think he would be if he did all of those things? Would he turn into a girl?
18 GEORGE: Mmm ...
19 B.D.: (reads about Oliver going to dancing school) Was that a good idea?
20 GEORGE: Yep.
21 B.D.: Why was that a good idea?
22 GEORGE: Because he needs the exercise ...
23 B.D.: Why did they say sissy to him?
24 GEORGE: Because he thinks, they think he's a boy.
25 B.D.: And so if he's a boy, isn't he allowed to dance?
26 GEORGE: Uh uh. (shakes head) ...
27 B.D.: (reads about boys crossing out 'sissy' and writing 'star') So why did they do that?
28 GEORGE: Because he was a good dancer.
29 B.D.: So do they like him now?
30 GEORGE: Yup.
31 B.D.: Yup. And so is that going to be good? A good ending?
32 GEORGE: Yeah.

33 B.D.: Yeah. And so, do you ever like to do girl things?
34 GEORGE: No.
35 B.D.: No? Do you like to play with girls sometimes?
36 GEORGE: Yup.
37 B.D.: What sort of things do you like to play with girls?
38 GEORGE: Um, just play.
39 B.D.: Just play?
40 GEORGE: Mmm.
41 B.D.: Do you like to play with teddy bears and dollies and prams and things?
42 GEORGE: No, I don't play with dollies. I just play with my very funny teddy bears.
43 B.D.: You play with your teddy bears do you?
44 GEORGE: Yup. They're funny.
45 B.D.: And tell me what you do with your teddy bears.
46 GEORGE: Sometimes they do somersaults.
47 B.D.: Do they?
48 Geroge: Yeah, and they do backflips.
49 B.D.: And sometimes do you feed your teddy bear in the highchair?
50 GEORGE: I don't have, I only have Braddy's highchair. I can put him in.
51 B.D.: Right, would you like to do that?
(We then discuss all of the things that Oliver did and George claims that these are all boy's things except for paper dolls.)
52 B.D.: So would you ever play with paper dolls?
53 GEORGE: No.
54 B.D.: If I gave you a really, really good set of paper dollies with paper dresses, would you play with them sometimes when you were by yourself and no-one was watching? Would you?
55 GEORGE: Yep.
56 B.D.: And would you do it if someone was watching?
57 GEORGE: No ...
58 B.D.: What would be a girl thing that you would really like to do?
59 GEORGE: Nothing.
60 B.D.: Nothing? You can't think of any girl things that you would really like to do?
61 GEORGE: No.
62 B.D.: What about pretending to be a mother?
63 GEORGE: Ah, no.
64 B.D.: No, you wouldn't like to do that?
65 GEORGE: Uh uh (shakes head)
66 B.D.: OK. What about dressing up. Is that a girl thing or a boy thing or both?
67 GEORGE: Both.
68 B.D.: Uh huh. Right. But his dad doesn't think that, does he? His dad thinks that they're all girl things?
69 GEORGE: Yes.
70 B.D.: Is his dad right or wrong?
71 GEORGE: Right.
72 B.D.: His dad's right?
73 GEORGE: Yep.

131

74 B.D.:   Why is his dad right? 'Cause we think that they're girl things and boy things but his dad thinks that they're just boy things. And do you think that his dad's right?
75 GEORGE: Yes.
76 B.D.:   So he disagrees with us and he's right?
77 GEORGE: Yeah.
78 B.D.:   Well I think we're right. I think that we think that boys can do those things.
79 GEORGE: Mmm. But that's a funny thing. (pointing to picture)
80 B.D.:   It is a funny lamp, isn't it?
81 GEORGE: Mmm.
82 B.D.:   So are daddies right all the time?
83 GEORGE: Yeah . . .
84 B.D.:   So can mummies be wrong?
85 GEORGE: Yep.
86 B.D.:   Can daddies be wrong?
87 GEORGE: No. They can be right.
88 B.D.:   They can be right? And they can't be wrong?
89 GEORGE: Uh uh. (shakes head)

George sees sex as mutable (16−18). Behaving like a girl means that you will become a girl. He admits to liking girls' things (2, 8, 50−1) but doesn't call them girls' things, asserting that they are also appropriate for boys (34, 59, 63, 66). He nevertheless draws the line at paper dolls, at least in public, and denies liking to play with dollies, showing that he does have boundaries to his categories of boy and girl. While this might seem to suggest that George has achieved a softening of the boundaries and a move in the right direction, I would suggest, rather, a very deep level of tension — what he believes or experiences must be wrong if a male parent says that it is wrong. Male adults thus have access, as far as George is concerned, to some infallible way of knowing (71, 75, 77, 82, 87−9), which overrides what he and I think is right (74, 76, 78). Children and female adults (84−5) are fallible. Despite George's clear preference in his play for things that are normally seen as for girls, he has established the duality in his thinking quite 'correctly' — the man is the one who knows, the woman the one who is or can be wrong, who doesn't really know. Women and children, apparently, do not have access to 'masculine' knowledge, and George and I are potentially always in the wrong, first for believing that it is alright for boys to do these things and second, in George's case, for doing them. His compromises include treating his teddy like soccer ball and throwing it around, combining heavy disciplinarian and protective elements in his nurturant play, and focusing on heroes like Rita the Rescuer who have 'male' superpowers and yet who do not compromise their 'femininity'. These compromises are not acceptable to the other children and so George must often be alone and choose sympathetic women to talk to, who share this 'fallibility'.

Thus, even though children like Joanne and George seem to be moving to the margins and beyond and thereby challenging the dualistic nature of the categories, they are deeply constrained by them. Their resistance leads them to a contradictory set of understandings about their own identity that is a springboard for self-rejection as well as (in Joanne's case) adulation of the other sex and (in George's case) adulation of the male who 'knows'. These children do not simply want to be like the 'opposite' sex. They want to be able to position themselves in a range of ways that includes what we currently understand as 'masculine' and 'feminine' ways but without a privileging of one over the other.

Challenging the dualism

Within the framework through which most children appear to interpret gender, 'masculinity' equals not-'femininity' and vice versa. Discouraging children from positioning themselves as 'masculine' or 'feminine' generally means encouraging 'home corner' behaviour in boys and macho behaviour in girls, and discouraging the reverse. Childen often interpret such pressures from adults as confused, and the adults in question in need of category-maintenance work done on them. Connell et al. suggest that if we get enough so-called deviants, the categories will shift so that what is taken to be normal is what was once taken to be deviant. Certainly this is the hope of many feminists whose everyday practice involves shifting the conceptual frameworks of the individuals they interact with in the hope that they will come to see as normal that which they originally found peculiar or threatening. This strategy is one of broadening the definition of 'masculine' and 'feminine' so that they are no longer bipolar, but rather bimodal—two ways of being that partially overlap.

I believe this does not go far enough, however, because as long as the dualism is kept intact, category-maintenance work will be done around the people who do not stay in their proper 'mode'.

I would suggest that a more constructive direction to move in with individual children and groups of children is to encourage them to distinguish between genital/reproductive sex (maleness and femaleness) and the range of 'masculine' and 'feminine' positionings that they are free to take up without violating or calling in question their genital sex. As well, it is important that we distinguish between the taking up of various positionings and the individual identity of the child. The fact that a boy takes up a macho/superhero position does not mean that he is incapable of taking up other apparently contradictory positionings when this becomes appropriate. Children should be free to explore the full range of positionings currently available within our narrative and interactive structures, and be free to develop new ones as they learn what it means to dissociate genital reproductive sex from personal and social being, and to find ways of thinking about and describing their own and other's behaviour independently of what we currently think of as 'masculine' and 'feminine'.

My own first attempt to imagine what life would be like not locked into the female half of the male-female dualism was through a visual image rather than words written on a page. I then attempted to capture the essence of that image as follows:

It was cool and peaceful by the pond. The fountain in the middle of the pond was soothing, the ducks graceful. Sadly I noticed that the water of the pond was muddy and opaque—the filtered sunlight was not able to penetrate even its surface—as if a skin lay over the top. But as I stared at the water I noticed the reflection on the surface of the water—a silver rippling pattern created by the fountain. Then I noticed that the silver ripples were the reflected sky visible through the canopy of leaves above. The murky depths had disappeared and in my transfixed gaze was a silver and green picture of extraordinary depth and beauty. I could switch my gaze from the opaque, brown impenetrable surface—which seemed, like male ("phallogocentric") knowledge, to lead nowhere and to be of no great beauty—to the reflected depth of the sky, there in the exact same place as the murky brown, but of breathtaking brilliance, imaging exactly the excitement I feel at these new insights into the unnatural constraints of 'knowledge' as that term is usually understood.

—the reflection: shimmering, moving, constantly broken up but always there—the depth is the sky but I see it by peering downward.
—the pool: the man-made object—beautiful in its own way and part of the vision, even potentiating the vision, but the vision is only gained through disattending the pool.

By looking directly at the heart of the fountain I can see both.

The opaque pool held me at a distance, kept me separate, identifiably me as a separate being sitting by the pond—the reflection drew me in, enveloped me, made me feel at home, at ease, known and knowable, not any longer an isolated being sitting at the edge of a pond.

These two ways of knowing and being are both mine. If I construe one as somehow 'masculine' and the other 'feminine', then I am both simultaneously 'masculine' and 'feminine' and separately 'masculine' and 'feminine'. In the reflected image I lose myself, my corporal image as other to any person, and I am sexless, neither male nor female.

In struggling beyond the categories I use them still to say what it is that I am. I am both excited at the experience of myself as neither male nor female and excited by the possibility of deconstructing what I have come to see as 'masculine' ways of seeing and knowing. These 'masculine' ways of knowing have been central in my oppression because the very capacity to see from a 'masculine' perspective allows me to see myself as inadequate, lacking, the opposite to the knower, the female who cannot know (Davies, 1988b; Smith, 1979).

Yet at the same time those very 'masculine' forms and ways of knowing form a large part of the symbolism and structure that allow me to subvert and go beyond them, that inspire me to say what I am and am not (cf. Irigaray, 1985). I cannot be simply male or female, except in a limited reproductive sense, since I am both, my experience of one or the other depending on the way I am thinking, or the subject position that I take up or that is made available to me through the various discourses in which I participate. Ultimately I can be both or neither. The possession of female genitalia has meant that I have had most access to the forms of discourse in which I am female, object, other to a male. On the other hand, the possession of one set of genitalia rather than another has not precluded the imaginative construction of a positive self who is an active subject, nor action based on that imagining, though the material world has often intervened to make the action based on those active, agentic positions more difficult (Davies, 1988b).

Despite the fact that maleness and femaleness need only be relevant to reproduction, the significance of maleness and femaleness has been extended far beyond the reproductive function. Reproduction itself has been extended to include care for and nurture of young, as if this were part of the biological package that comes with the biological fact of females carrying the foetus while it develops. Amongst monkeys, at least, babies who have not been mothered themselves display no 'natural' ability to mother and generally reject their own babies, suggesting that mothering is almost completely a learned behaviour. The idea of opposite bipolar sexes has also been extended into sexuality, 'natural' sex being associated with potentially reproductive (penetrative, heterosexual) sex between males and females. That there are people who find themselves attracted to people who happen to have the same genitals as themselves has not really challenged the widespread belief that the sexes are opposite and that that opposition is what makes them attractive, and that attraction is what the perpetuation of the human race depends on.

If the dualism were rejected and people were free to position themselves as a person in terms of their interests and abilities quite independently of the set of genitals they happen to have, and were free to dress and move through the world without being obliged to mark themselves up as male or female, then there would still be many people who would recognisably be what we now think of as female or male, and there would be many who were not. They would not simply be marking themselves as the 'other' sex (though some might), but presenting and positioning themselves in ways that mark neither maleness nor femaleness. It is interesting and amusing to think of the different social strategies that would have to be developed by committed heterosexual and homosexual people to establish that they were correctly orienting their presexual behaviour towards a person with the appropriate set of genitals, where genital sex has ceased to be central to identity in the everyday world.

Already there is a great deal of variety amongst people. Masculinities and femininities vary in the same way as, say, intelligence, though intelligence has been subjected to similar political processes which simplify the actual complexity and divide it into two apparent camps. The social world cannot really be divided into bright and dull people, though people are constituted through discourse in that way. There are people who are interesting and competent in a variety of ways, and those same people are boring or dull or incompetent in a different set of ways. Although the makers and users of IQ tests would have us think that intelligence can be measured in a linear fashion, it is only very limited aspects of school-based competence that can be measured in this way. Because of the power of the school system to control people's lives and to shape the ways that they think about themselves, IQ or school-based competence, or lack of competence, has been given far more weight than it should. 'Brightness' is neither unitary nor linear, nor a fixed feature of persons any more than 'stupidity' is. The same argument can be made in relation to beauty and ugliness, or almost any other feature of persons. There are some features like height and weight that can be measured on a linear continuum, but these should not be used as analogues for features such as intelligence, beauty or gender, which are socially constructed bipolarities involving both the *reduction* of a complex array of features into a simplistic dualistic system, and the *location* of those features in the person.

So how are we to move beyond the male–female dualism? The simple answer is that all we have to do is to stop doing the work that maintains the difference. That, of course, is more easily said than done. Individual identities are already organised around the idea of the sex/gender difference and the language and social structure cannot easily be changed through individual acts of resistance. It is nevertheless possible to work towards discursive and interactive practices in which genital sex and identity in the everyday world are separated, and in which, therefore, individuals are under no kind of obligation to mark up their sex so that it is readable by others, in which there is no political advantage to being marked as male rather than female, in which any kind of human activity including that which has previously been associated with one sex can be taken up by any individual if that is where their interest lies. The challenge is to learn to think and to desire not in terms of the male–female dualism, but in terms of the existing variety and complexity of positionings available to persons. This can only take place through the development of discursive practices and narrative forms through which that recognition and those new positionings are recognised as meaningful and legitimate. As Harré says, 'The task of the re-construction of society can be taken up by anyone at any time in any face to face encounter' (1979:405). But the trick is to have others recognise and accept the discourse through which the reconstruction is taking place (cf. Davies, 1989 and forthcoming).

Conclusion

At the heart of the *idea* of maleness seems to be the idea of power as male power, with females having power only in the domestic realm or as helpers of men in the male sphere. The knowledge of this is embedded in the narrative structures of books and of play, in the very discursive practices through which each child's identity is formulated and sustained. This knowledge becomes embedded in the bodies of the children, not only through their physical practices which affect their musculature, but through the attitudes they develop towards themselves either as active agents who can and should act powerfully in the public sphere, or as sexualised beings whose agency is profoundly inhibited through the positioning of themselves as the passive recipients of another's gaze.

If we think of the person in liberal humanist terms, that is, with a unitary and coherent identity formed during childhood, and who comes to know him/herself in relation to a real and knowable world through a rational apprehension of lived experience, using language to give expression to that experience, then we must leave the children where they are, with their subjectivities formulated around their knowledge of the 'natural' division of the social world into male and female persons, one and only one of which they are. The only changes that can take place within this model are at the first and second of Kristeva's tiers; that is, we can keep pushing for females to have access in the male sphere and we can attempt to remove the stigma from 'femininity'. The essence of the male-female dualism, however, is that power resides in the male. The power imbalance will go on being constituted through any discourse which holds the dualism intact. Equal opportunity programmes and non-sexist child raising conceived at Kristeva's first and second tiers are necessarily limited in the degree of change they can bring about.

But language does not simply reflect a fixed world 'out there'. 'Language offers a range of ways of interpreting our lives ... In the process of interacting with the world, we give meaning to things by learning the linguistic processes of thought and speech, drawing on

138

the ways of understanding the world to which we have access'
(Weedon, 1987:85). And in each of the forms of discourse that we
currently use, and which we can develop we constitute ourselves and
our subjectivity in subtly or sometimes radically different ways.
Each discourse that I participate in constitutes me differently,
empowers or constrains me, depending on the assumptions
embedded in it about what I can or cannot do, think, feel or be. It
also determines how I think change might take place.

One liberating aspect of poststructuralist through is that it allows
me to recognise the multiple discourses in which I participate and to
see myself differently constituted through each of them. It allows
me to imagine a discourse in which I can position myself as neither
male nor female, but human. It also allows me to see fully, for the
first time, the extent of my entrapment in known discourses.

More importantly, it allows me to focus on the contradictions in
my experience, not as failures of rational thought but as the creative
source of new understanding, new discourses.

This allows me to engage in liberal feminist discourse, radical
feminist discourse as well as poststructuralist discourse without feeling anxious about the contradictions between these. It is no longer
my moral duty as a human being to achieve an integrated and unitary
set of explanations for my thoughts and feelings (which was necessary
to have credibility as a person within liberal humanist discourse).
Rather, it becomes possible to locate myself as adopting a variety of
discursive practices depending on the context, the interactive others
and the task at hand. Sometimes I will engage in liberal feminist
discourse when it is clear that the issue is one of unjust exclusion on
the basis of sex. At other times I will celebrate being female on the
basis of my own experience and the experiences of my female
friends and colleagues. At other times I will feel free and powerful
enough to move beyond these to a set of interactive and discursive
practices in which the metaphysical nature of 'male' and 'female' is
clear to me and to those with whom I live out the new narrative
structures and metaphors of my life.

These freedoms should also be available to children. When they
wish to behave in 'sex-appropriate' ways, that is, in contexts where
nothing else will be understood as meaningful behaviour, or where
such behaviour has some positive value, they should feel free to do
so. Parents and teachers who feel they have failed each time boys
are aggressive or girls are 'prissy' should simply accept that the child
has judged at this point in time that that is the most appropriate or
comfortable way to behave. Similarly, children should be free to
take up positionings that are now associated with the other sex
through gaining access to a discourse in which the possession of a
particular set of genitals does not limit one to 'masculine' and
'feminine' positionings. That discourse I have attempted to elaborate

in this book, and it can be made available to children through feminist stories, through play and through developing a capacity to see dualistic discourse as just that—one way of construing the world.

Children are subjected to the material force of the discursive and interactive practices through which the male—female dualism is constituted as a given. They can learn, however, to see this as one form of discourse that they are free to resist if they are freed from the moral obligation to constitute themselves in terms of a polar definition based on genital/reproductive sex. For those who might think that it is too difficult for children to take on the fact of multiple discourses and their associated realities, I would like to point out two things:

1 Children struggle for quite a long time to learn the liberal humanist concept of the person as fixed and unitary, since this does not adequately capture their experience which is of multiple, diverse and contradictory ways of being (Davies, 1982). To articulate that experience of diversity as normal and acceptable could be quite empowering for them, and save them from the awful task of trying to render rational and consistent that which is not so.

2 Children display an ease in moving from one discursive framework to another and are not affronted by others doing so, though they do recognise the need for reciprocity of perspectives, that is, that people who are interacting with each other need to be adopting the same discursive structure.

In relation to the reading and writing of feminist stories, this acceptance of diversity is also important. Characters such as Elizabeth are both 'feminine *and* heroic. She is no more the fictional unified character of liberal humanist thought than I am or the children are. Heroes and other fictional characters do not have to be designed so that children can identify with them wholly, though they do have to fire the imagination sufficiently that one can, for the duration of the story, see the world and experience the world as it is experienced by them. As an adult reader of *The Paper Bag Princess*, for example, I find much in Elizabeth's experience that I can identify with. I follow her adventure with close attention and I feel her anger and rejoice in the freedom at the end. In order to do this I need to ignore the fact that she persuades the dragon to devastate whole forests in order to retrieve Ronald. I also feel somewhat uncomfortable with the fact that she uses 'feminine' wiles to trick the dragon, though her trickery is not necessarily to be interpreted negatively since it is not unlike Puss in Boots' strategies with the giant. Her foolishness in loving someone so patently unworthy as Ronald and her capacity in the end to recognise that and to walk away are the salient features for me. This is not altogether different from Robbie's ability to make Ronald's gold medal, and the fact that Ronald does not love Elizabeth the salient features which mean that Elizabeth is a nuisance that Ronald is better off without.

Let us return, then, to the point where we began. Why does it matter so much to children that they get their own and other people's gender right? Why do current programmes for change have so little effect? Essentially the answer lies in the fact that within the discursive practices made available to children, the only comprehensible identity available to them is as 'boy' or 'girl', 'male' or 'female'. These are constituted not just as two amongst many possible categories but as two exclusive categories which take their meaning in relation to each other. It is made clear to the children through the form of the language with which they come to know the world that having a particular set of genitals is not enough to signify one's position as male or female. Being identifiably male or female involves one in particular ways of being, and specific kinds of positionings in lived and imagined narrative structures. It is always the 'opposite' sex that is so constituted, not merely an 'other'.

Children need to be given access to a discourse which frees them from the burden of the liberal humanist obligations of coming to know a fixed reality in which they have a unified and rationally coherent identity separate and distinct from the social world. They can gain this freedom through an acknowledgement of the ways in which each form of discursive practice constitutes them differently. At the same time, they need access to forms of discursive practice where their social practice is not defined in terms of the set of genitals they happen to have. They need to have access to imaginary worlds in which new metaphors, new forms of social relations, and new patterns of power and desire are explored. They need the freedom to position themselves in multiple ways, some of which will be recognisably 'feminine', some 'masculine' as we currently understand these terms, and some totally unrelated to current discursive practices. Eventually we may come to see these terms, 'masculine' and 'feminine', as archaic and wonder how the social world could ever have been reduced to two types of people, these types being related to relatively minor pieces of anatomy whose sole relevance lies in biological reproduction. In such a Utopia those masculine and feminine qualities that are worthy of celebration would still be able to be celebrated, but without the destructive marginalisation of the feminine and without the restrictions currently placed on people to be exclusively or primarily one or the other.

Appendix—Feminist and non-sexist stories

Realistic stories about gender set in the domestic and/or school setting

1 With an explicit feminist message

Brown, A. (1986) *Piggybook* London: Julia MacRae Books
de Paola, T. (1981) *Oliver Button Is a Sissy* London: Methuen
Mack, B. and Buchanan, M. (1979) *Jesse's Dream Skirt* Chapel Hill, NC: Lollipop Power Inc.
Yeoman, J. and Blake, Q. (1979) *The Wild Washerwomen* Harmondsworth: Puffin Books

2 With no explicit feminist message but with non-sexist content

Bang, M. (1983) *Ten, Nine, Eight* London: Julia MacRae Books
Brandenburg, F. (1983) *Aunt Nina and her Nephews and Nieces* London: The Bodley Head
Cooney, B. (1982) *Miss Rumphius* London: Julia MacRae Books
Cox, D. (1985) *Bossyboots* London: The Bodley Head
Denton, K. (1985) *Felix and Alexander* Oxford: Oxford University Press
Eichler, M. (1971) *Martin's Father* Chapel Hill, NC: Lollipop Power Inc.
Gaspar, T. (1974) *Yolanda's Hike* Berkeley: New Seed Press
Smyth, G. and James, A. (1981) *A Pet for Mrs Arbuckle* Gosford: Ashton Scholastic
Suroweicki, S. and Lenthall, P. (1977) *Joshua's Day* Chapel Hill, NC: Lollipop Power Inc.
Williams, V. (1981) *Three Days on a River on a Red Canoe* New York: Mulberry Books.
———— (1982) *A Chair for My Mother* New York: Mulberry Books
———— (1983) *Something Special for Me* New York: Mulberry Books

Realistic stories about gender using animals instead of people

1 With an explicit feminist message

Turin, A. and Bosnia, N. (1976a) *A Fortunate Catastrophe* London: Writers and Readers Publishing Cooperative

—— (1976b) *Arthur and Clementine* London: Writers and Readers Publishing Cooperative

—— (1976c) *Sugarpink Rose* London: Writers and Readers Publishing Cooperative.

2 With no explicit feminist message but with non-sexist content

Armitage, R. and D (1978) *'Don't Forget Matilda!'* London: André Deutsch.

Tompert, A. (1976) *Little Fox Goes to the End of the World* New York: Scholastic Inc.

Wells, R. (1973) *Benjamin and Tulip* Harmondsworth: Kestrel Books

Fantasy stories in which people are given extraordinary powers

1 Feminist retellings of traditional stories

Cole, B (1986) *Princess Smartypants* London: Hamish Hamilton

—— (1987a) *Prince Cinders* London: Heinemann

Vesey, A. *The Princess and the Frog* Harmondsworth: Puffin Books

2 New feminist stories woven out of some elements of the old but introducing a new narrative form

Cole, B. (1985) *The Trouble with Mum* London: Heinemann

—— (1987b) *The Trouble with Gran* London: Heinemann

Coles, D. (1983) *The Clever Princess* London: Sheba Feminist Publishers

de Paola, T. (1980) *The Knight and the Dragon* London: Methuen

Dugan, M. and Hicks, A. (1980) *Dragon's Breath* Melbourne: Puffin Books

Munsch, R. and Marchenko, M. (1980) *The Paper Bag Princess* Toronto: Annick Press Ltd

Offen, H. (1981) *Rita the Rescuer* London: Methuen

Wood, A. (1981) *The Princess and the Dragon* Child's Play (International) Ltd

Collections of stories for slightly older children

Corbalis, J. and Craig, H. (1987) *The Wrestling Princess and Other Stories* London: Knight Books

Johnston Phelps, E. (ed.) (1978) *Tatterhood and Other Tales* New York: Feminist Press

Lee, T. (1983) *Red as Blood or Tales from the Sisters Grimmer* New York: Daw Books Inc.

Pogrebin, L. (ed.) (1982) *Stories for Free Children* McGraw Hill

Williams, J. (1978) *The Practical Princess and Other Liberating Fairy Tales* London: The Bodley Head

Zipes, J. (1986) *Don't Bet on the Prince: Contemporary Feminist Fairy Tales in North America and England* Aldershot: Gower. (There is an extensive bibliography of some hundreds of feminist stories in this book.)

Bibliography

Adams, J. (1986) *The Conspiracy of the Text* Boston: Routledge & Kegan Paul

Adams, C. and Walkerdine, V. (1986) *Investigating Gender in the Primary School: Activity Based Inset Materials for Primary Teachers* London: Inner London Education Authority

Aiken, J. (1971) *The Kingdom under the Sea* Harmondsworth: Puffin

Anti-sexist Working Party (1985) '"Look, Jane, look": Anti-sexist Initiatives in Primary Schools' in G. Weiner (ed.) *Just a Bunch of Girls: Feminist Approaches to Schooling* Milton Keynes: Open University Press

Anyon, J. (1983) 'Intersections of Gender and Class: Accommodation and Resistance by Working Class and Affluent Females to Contradictory Sex-role Ideologies' In S. Walker and L. Barton (eds) *Gender, Class and Education* London: Falmer Press

Applebee, A. (1978) *The Child's Concept of Story* Chicago: University of Chicago Press

Armitage, R. and D. (1978) '*Don't Forget Matilda*' London: André Deutsch

Baker, C. and Davies, B. (forthcoming) 'A Lesson on Sex Roles' *Gender and Education* 1 (1)

Bang, M. (1983) *Ten, Nine, Eight* London: Julia MacRae Books

Bateson, G. (1982) 'A Theory of Play and Fantasy' in E. Bredo, and W. Feinberg, (eds) *Knowledge and Values in Educational Research* Philadelphia: Temple University Press

Beloff, H. (1980) 'Are Models of Man Models of Women?' in A. Chapman, and D. Jones (eds) *Models of Man* London: The British Psychological Society

Black, M. and Coward, R. (1981) 'Linguistic, Social and Sexual Relations' *Screen Education* 39

Bledsoe, J. (1977–78) 'The World of the Cave Kid: The Rightful Recognition of Children's Knowledge' *Interchange* 8, pp. 1–2

Brandenburg, F. (1983) *Aunt Nina and her Nephews and Nieces* London: The Bodley Head

Browne, A. (1986) *Piggybook* London: Julia MacRae Books

Bruce, W. (1985) 'The Implications of Stereotyping in the First Years of School' *Australian Journal of Early Childhood* 10 (2)

Bussey, K. (1986) 'The First Socialisation' In N. Grieve, and A. Burns (eds) *Australian Women: New Feminist Perspectives* Melbourne: Oxford University Press

Bibliography

Cameron, D. (1985) *Feminism and Linguistic Theory* London: Macmillan

Clark, M. (forthcoming) *The Great Divide: The Construction of Gender in the Primary School* Canberra: Curriculum Development Centre

Clarricoates, K. (1979) The Theft of Girls' Creativity, unpublished paper cited in Mahoney, P. (1983)

Cole, B. (1985) *The Trouble with Mum* London: Heinemann

—— (1986) *Princess Smartypants* London: Hamish Hamilton

—— (1987a) *Prince Cinders* London: Heinemann

—— (1987b) *The Trouble with Gran* London: Heinemann

Coles, D. (1983) *The Clever Princess* London: Sheba Feminist Publishers

Connell, R. W. (1983) *Which Way Is Up? Essays on Class, Sex and Culture* Sydney: Allen & Unwin

—— Connell, B., Radican, N. and Martin, P. (1987) The Changing Faces of Masculinity Sydney: Macquarie University (unpublished paper)

Conney, B. (1982) *Miss Rumphius* London: Julia MacRae Books

Corbalis, J. and Craig, H. (1987) *The Wrestling Princess and Other Stories* London: Knight Books

Corsaro, W. (1979) '"We're Friends Right?" Children's Use of Access Rituals in a Nursery School' *Language in Society* 8

Cox, D. (1985) *Bossyboots* London: The Bodley Head

Cranny-Francis, A. (1988) 'Out among the Stars in a Red Shift: Women and Science Fiction' *Australian Feminist Studies* 6

Crapo, L. (1985) *Hormones: The Messengers of Life* New York: W. H. Freeman and Co.

Davies, B. (1982) *Life in the Classroom and Playground: The Accounts of Primary School Children* London: Routledge & Kegan Paul

—— (1983a) *Towards Non-sexist Language* Melbourne: FAUSA

—— (1983b) 'The Role Pupils Play in the Social Construction of Classroom Order' *British Journal of Sociology of Education* 4 (1)

—— (1987) 'The Accomplishment of Genderedness in Preschool Aged Children,' in A. Pollard (ed.) *Children and their Primary Schools* London: Falmer Press

—— (1988a) *Gender Equity and Early Childhood* Canberra: Commonwealth Schools Commission

—— (1988b) Romantic Love and Women's Sexuality, unpublished paper

Davies, B. (1989) 'Education for sexism. A theoretical analysis of the sex gender bias in education' *Educational Philosophy and Theory* 21 (1)

Davies, B. (forthcoming) 'The discursive production of the male/female dualism in school settings' *Oxford Review of Education*

de Beauvoir, S. (1972) *The Second Sex* Harmondsworth: Penguin

Denton, K. (1985) *Felix and Alexander* Oxford: Oxford University Press

de Paola, T. (1980) *The Knight and the Dragon* London: Methuen

—— (1981) *Oliver Button Is a Sissy* London: Methuen

Dugan, M and Hicks, A. (1980) *Dragon's Breath* Melbourne: Puffin Books

Edwards, A. (1983) 'Sex Roles: A Problem for the Sociology of Women' *The Australian and New Zealand Journal of Sociology* 19 (3)

Eichler, M. (1971) *Martin's Father* Chapel Hill, NC: Lollipop Power Inc.

Favat, A. (1977) *Child and Tale: The Origins of Interest* Urbana

Freebody, P. and Baker, C. (1987) 'The Construction and Operation of Gender in Children's First School Books' in A. Pauwels (ed.) *Women*

Language and Society in Australia and New Zealand Sydney: Australian Professional Publications

Garfinkel, H. (1967) *Studies in Ethnomethodology* Englewood Cliffs: Prentice Hall

Garnica, O. (1979) 'The Boys Have the Muscles and the Girls Have the Sexy Legs: Adult–child Speech and the Use of Generic Person Labels' in O. Garnica, and M. King, *Language, Children and Society: The Effect of Social Factors on Children Learning to Communicate* Oxford: Pergamon Press

Gaspar, T. (1974) *Yolanda's Hike* Berkeley: New Seed Press

Gilligan, C. (1982) *In a Different Voice: Psychological Theory and Women's Development* Cambridge, Mass.: Harvard University Press

Goldman, R. and Goldman, J. (1982) *Children's Sexual Thinking* London: Routledge & Kegan Paul.

Gross, E. (1986a) 'What Is Feminist Theory?' in C. Pateman and E. Gross (eds) *Feminist Challenges: Social and Political Theory* Sydney: Allen & Unwin

—— (1986b) Inscriptions and Body Maps: Representations and the Corporeal, paper presented to the *Masculine/Feminine/Representation Conference*, Sydney

Harré, R. (1979) *Social Being* Oxford: Blackwell

—— (1985) The Language Game of Self Ascription: A Note' in K. Gergen and K. Davis (eds) *The Social Construction of the Person* New York: Springer-Verlag

Haug, F. (1984) 'Morals Also Have Two Genders' *New Left Review* 143

—— (ed.) (1987) *Female Sexualization* Erica Carter (trans.) London: Verso

Henriques, J., Hollway, W., Urwin, C., Venn, C. and Walkerdine, V. (1984) *Changing the Subject: Psychology, Social Regulation and Subjectivity* London: Methuen

Herzberger, S. and Tennen, H. (1985) '"Snips and Snails and Puppy Dog Tails": Gender of Agent, Recipient, and Observer as Determinants of Perceptions of Discipline' *Sex Roles* 12 (7/8)

Houston, B. (1985) 'Gender Freedom and the Subtleties of Sexist Education' *Educational Theory* 35 (4)

Irigaray, L. (1985) *This Sex Which Is not One* Ithaca: Cornell University Press

Jackson, S. (1982) *Childhood and Sexuality* Oxford: Blackwell

Johnston Phelps, E. (ed.) (1987) *Tatterhood and Other Tales* New York: The Feminist Press

Kennard, J. (1986) 'A Theory for Lesbian Readers' in E. Flynn and P. Schweickart (eds) *Gender and Reading* (Baltimore: The Johns Hopkins University Press

Kenway, J. and Willis, S. (1986) Girls, Self-esteem and Education: From the Personal to the Political and from the Universal to the Specific, paper presented to the AARE Conference, Melbourne

Kessler, S., Ashendon, D., Connell, B. and Dowsett, G. (1982) *Ockers and Disco-maniacs* Sydney: Inner City Education Centre

Kessler, S. and McKenna, W. (1978) *Gender: An Ethnomethodological Approach* Chicago: University of Chicago Press

Kristeva, J. (1981) 'Women's Time' A. Jardine (trans.) *Signs* 7 (1), reprinted (1986a) in T. Moi (ed.) *The Kristeva Reader* Oxford: Blackwell

Kristeva, J. (1986b) *Tales of Love* New York: Columbia University Press

Leahey, T. (1987) *'Pedofile Relationships: Positive and voluntary Experiences'* mimeograph, Sydney: University of Sydney

Lee, T. (1983) *Red as Blood or Tales from the Sisters Grimmer* New York: Daw Books Inc.

Lees, S. (1986a) 'A New Approach to the Study of Girls' *Youth and Policy* 16

—— (1986b) *Losing Out: Sexuality and Adolescent Girls* London: Hutchinson

Lunneborg, P. (1982) 'Role Model Influences of Non-traditional Professional Women' *Journal of Vocational Behaviour* 20

Maccoby, E. and Jacklin, C. (1974) *The Psychology of Sex Differences* Stanford: Stanford University Press

Mack, B. and Buchanan, M. (1979) *Jesse's Dream Skirt* Chapel Hill, NC; Lollipop Power Inc.

Mahoney, P. (1983) 'How Alice's Chin Really Came to Be Pressed against Her Foot: Sexist Processes of Interaction in Mixed-sex classrooms' *Women's Studies International Forum* 6 (1)

Mehan, H. and Wood. H. (1975) *The Reality of Ethnomethodology* New York: Wiley

Moi, T. (1985) *Sexual Textual Politics* London: Methuen

—— (1986) 'Feminist literary criticism' in A. Jefferson and D. Robey (eds) *Modern Literary Theory* London: Batsford.

Munsch, R. and Martchenko, M. (1980) *The Paper Bag Princess* Toronto: Annick Press Ltd

Offen, H. (1981) *Rita the Rescuer* London: Methuen

Pogrebin, L. (1982) *Stories for Free Chidren*

Radway, J. (1984) *Reading the Romance* London: Verso

Rogers, L. (1975) 'Biology and Human Behaviour' in J. Mercer (ed.) *The Other Half: Women in Australian Society* Harmondsworth: Penguin

—— (1981) 'Biology: Gender Differentiation and Sexual Variation' in N. Grieve and P. Grimshaw (eds) *Australian Women: Feminist Perspectives* Melbourne: Oxford University Press

—— (1988) 'Biology, the Popular Weapon: Sex Differences in Cognitive Function' in B. Caine, E. Grosz and M. de Leppervanche (eds) *Crossing Boundaries: Feminisms and the Critique of Knowledges* Sydney: Allen & Unwin

Rose, R., Gordon, T. and Bernstein, I. (1972) 'Plasma Testosterone Levels in the Male Rhesus: Influences of Sexual and Social Stimuli' *Science* 178

Rubin, G. (1975) 'The Traffic in Women: Notes on the Political Economy of Sex' in P. R. Reiter (ed.) *Toward an Anthropology of Women* New York: Monthly Review

Safilios-Rothschild, C. (1979) *Sex Role Socialisation and Sex Discrimination: A Bibliography* Washington: US Department of Health Education and Welfare

Sayers, J. (1986) *Sexual Contradictions: Psychology, Psychoanalysis and Feminism* London: Tavistock

Schweickart, P. (1986) 'Toward a Feminist Theory of Reading' in E. Flynn and P. Schweickart (eds) *Gender and Reading* Baltimore: The Johns Hopkins University Press

Silvers, R. (1979) Understanding Phenomenological Inquiry, paper presented to the Ontario Psychological Association Toronto

Smith, A. and Grimwood, S. (1983) 'Sex Role Stereotyping and Children's Concepts of Teachers and Principals' *Australian Journal of Early Childhood* 8 (2)

Smith, D. (1979) 'A Sociology for Women' in J. Sherman and E. Torton Beck *The Prism of Sex: Essays in the Sociology of Knowledge* Madison: The University of Wisconsin Press

Smyth, G. and James, A. (1981) *A Pet for Mrs Arbuckle* Gosford: Ashton Scholastic

Speier, M. (1976) 'The Child as Conversationalist: Some Culture Contact Features of Conversational Interactions between Adults and Children' in M. Hammersley and P. Woods *The Process of Schooling* London: Routledge & Kegan Paul

Stanley, L. and Wise, S. (1983) *Breaking Out: Feminist Consciousness and Feminist Research* London: Routledge & Kegan Paul

Steedman, C. (1985) 'Listen How the Caged Birds Sing: Amarjit's Song' in C. Steedman, V. Walkerdine and C. Urwin (eds) *Language, Gender and Childhood* London: Routledge & Kegan Paul

Strauss, E. W. (1966) 'The Upright Posture' in *Phenomenological Psychology* New York: Basic Books

Suleiman, S. (1986) (ed.) *The Female Body in Western Culture* Cambridge, Mass.: Harvard University Press

Suroweicki, S. and Lenthall, P. (1977) *Joshua's Day* Chapel Hill, NC: Lollipop Power Inc.

Threadgold, T. (1988) 'Language and Gender' *Australian Feminist Studies* 6

Tompert, A. (1976) *Little Fox Goes to the End of the World* New York: Scholastic Inc.

Turin, A. and Bosnia, N. (1976a) *A Fortunate Catastrophe* London: Writers and Readers Publishing Cooperative

—— (1976b) *Arthur and Clementine* London: Writers and Readers Publishing Cooperative

—— (1976c) *Sugarpink Rose* London: Writers and Readers Publishing Cooperative

Urburg, K. (1982) 'The Development of the Concepts of Masculinity and Femininity in Young Children' *Sex Roles* 8

Vesey, A. (1985) *The Princess and the Frog* Harmondsworth: Puffin Books

Waksler, F. (1986) 'Studying children: Phenomenological Insights' *Human Studies* 9

Walker, A. (1975) *Goodnight Willie Lee, I'll See You in the Morning* London: Women's Press

Walkerdine, V. (1981) 'Sex, Power and Pedagogy' *Screen Education* 38

—— (1984) 'Some Day my Prince Will Come' in A. McRobbie and M. Nava *Gender and Generation* London: Macmillan

—— (1985) 'On the Regulation of Speaking and Silence' in C. Steedman C. Urwin and V. Walkerdine (eds) *Language, Gender and Childhood* London: Routledge & Kegan Paul

Walkerdine, V. and Lucey, H. (1989) *Democracy in the Kitchen* London: Virago

Walum, L. R. (1977) *The Dynamics of Sex and Gender* London: Routledge & Kegan Paul

Weedon, C. (1987) *Feminist Practice and Poststructuralist Theory* Oxford: Blackwell

Weitzman, L. (1979) *Sex Role Socialisation* Palo Alto: Mayfield Publishing Co.

Wells. R. (1973) *Benjamin and Tulip* Harmondsworth: Kestrel Books

Wex, M. (1979) *Let's Take Back Our Space. Female and Male Body Language as a Result of Patriarchal Structures* Berlin: Frauenliteraturverlag Hermine Fees

Williams, J. (1978) *The Practical Princess and Other Liberating Fairy Tales* London: The Bodley Head

Williams, V. (1981) *Three Days on a river on a Red Canoe* New York: Mulberry Books

—— (1982) *A Chair for My Mother* New York: Mulberry Books

—— (1983) *Something Special for Me* New York: Mulberry Books

Wood, A. (1981) *The Princess and the Dragon* Child's Play (International) Ltd

Wyn, J. (1986) Schooling Work and Social Division: A Study of Working Class Youth, PhD thesis, Melbourne: Monash University

Yeoman, J. and Blake, Q. (1979) *The Wild Washerwomen* Harmondsworth: Puffin Books

Young, I. (1980) 'Throwing like a Girl: A Phenomenology of Body Comportment Motility and Spatiality' *Human Studies* 3

Zipes, J. (1982) 'The Potential of Liberating Fairy Stories for Children' *New Literary History* 13 (2)

—— (1986) *Don't Bet on the Prince: (Contemporary Feminist Fairy Tales in North America and England* Aldershot: Gower

Zuckerman, D. and Sayre, D. (1982) 'Cultural Sex-role Expectations and Children's Sex-role Concepts' *Sex Roles* 8

Index

Index

Herzberger S. and Tennen H., 15

inhibited intentionality, 18, 86
Irigaray L., 135

Jackson S., 5, 15, 120
Jesse's Dream Skirt, 19

Kennard J., 49
Kenway J. and Willis S., 7
Kessler, Ashendon, Connell and
    Dowsett, 63
Kessler and McKenna, x, 8, 9, 11
Kristeva J., 70–1, 138

Leahey T., 120
Lee T., 46
Lees S., 1, 77
Lunneborg P., 63

Maccoby E. and Jacklin C., 7
Mahoney P., 77, 85
male–female dualism, 48, 71, 81,
    109, 111–37
masculinity, 14, 49, 85, 88, 124–5,
    128–36
Mehan H. and Wood H., x
Moi T., 70, 71
moral order
    in stories, 27, 31, 43, 44, 46
    adult, 31, 50, 55, 72
motherhood, 78–85

narrative structures
    in children's play, 38–9, 41, 95–
    108
    in stories, 43, 56, 59, 68–9, 75,
    119
    in everyday life, 71, 72

Oliver Button is a Sissy, 27, 45, 48–
    54, 113–17, 124, 127, 128–9,
    130–2

Paper Bag Princess, The, xiii, 27,
    59–69, 73, 74, 75–7, 119, 120–1,
    122, 123, 124, 140

positioning, 2, 4, 12–20, 29, 45, 59,
    60, 85, 86, 90, 94–5, 138
poststructuralist theory, xi, 4, 6, 12
power
    adult, 4, 36
    male, 40, 44, 88–110
    female, 40, 44, 70–87, 118, 119,
    120
preschools
    description of, 22–5
    teachers' perceptions of children,
    86
    teacher–pupil interaction, 90
Princess and the Dragon, The, 31,
    54–6, 107, 118, 119, 122

Rita the Rescuer, 56–9, 107, 123
Rogers L., x, 9, 10
romantic mythology, 86, 121
Rose et al, 11

Safilios-Rothschild C., 7
Sayers J., 11
Schweickart P., 29
sex-role socialisation theory, 4–8
sexuality
    female, 77–8, 119–20, 121
    male, 77–8
Silvers R., 26
Smith D., 134
social structure, 12–13
Speier M., 5
Stanley L. and Wise S., 5
Steedman C., 22
stories
    feminist, 45–6, 47–8
    feminist analyses of, 45
    children's relation to, 47
Strauss E. W., 77

Threadgold T., 1

Urburg K., 63

Waksler F., 1, 5, 6
Walker, A., 74–5

Current books in Women's Studies